RIGHTS

by

ALAN R. WHITE

Ferens Professor of Philosophy
in the University of Hull

CLARENDON PRESS · OXFORD

Oxford University Press, Walton Street, Oxford OX2 6DP

Oxford New York Toronto
Delhi Bombay Calcutta Madras Karachi
Kuala Lumpur Singapore Hong Kong Tokyo
Nairobi Dar es Salaam Cape Town
Melbourne Auckland
and associated companies in
Beirut Berlin Ibadan Nicosia

Oxford is a trade mark of Oxford University Press

Published in the United States
by Oxford University Press, New York

First published 1984
Reprinted (new as paperback) 1985

British Library Cataloguing in Publication Data
White, Alan R.
  Rights.
  1. Rights (Philosophy)
  I. Title
  323.4'01   B105.R5
  ISBN 0-19-824716-8
  ISBN 0-19-824923-3

Library of Congress Cataloging in Publication Data
White, Alan R.
  Rights.
  Bibliography: p.
  Includes index.
  1. Natural law.   2. Duty.   I. Title.
  JC571.W425   1984   320'.01'1   84-1888
  ISBN 0-19-824716-8
  ISBN 0-19-824923-3

Printed in Great Britain
at the University Press, Oxford

W 29991 /6.95. 9.86

Acknowledgements

I am indebted to the editors and publishers of *Law and Philosophy*, *Modern Law Review*, *Archiv für Rechts- und Sozialphilosophie*, and of my book *Modal Thinking* (Blackwells) for permission to reuse material which I originally published with them. For helpful comments and criticisms on an earlier draft I thank most sincerely my colleagues at Hull, Edgar Page and David Walker in philosophy and Ray Smith in law, and my friend Neil MacCormick of Edinburgh.

Contents

1

Introduction

Rights are something we are all familiar with, whether we encounter them simply in wondering if we have any right to assume so and so or to expect such and such or in the rules and regulations of institutions and of games, or in pondering over weighty questions of morals, politics, or law. We frequently talk about, argue over, debate, assert, or deny our or others' rights. We may even fight and die for our own rights or attempt to trample on or extinguish those of others.

Rights are something one can have or be given, earn, enjoy, or exercise. They are something one can claim, demand, assert, insist on, or secure or what one can waive, surrender, relinquish, or forfeit. They can be recognized and protected or disregarded, altered, abridged, infringed, whittled away, violated, or destroyed.

What then is *a right* and how are we to understand the language of rights? It is these conceptual questions which I shall try to answer in this essay. I shall have nothing to say about what rights I think people actually have or ought to have.

(a) 'Right' as non-denotative

It is a natural assumption and was, indeed, a traditional philosophical assumption that all words are used in the same way as, for example, 'table', 'chair', 'body', 'arm', 'book', etc.; that is, to refer to some item in the world. Historically this seems also to have been true, at least in legal circles, of the word 'right'. So Pollock and Maitland tell us that in medieval times a right was regarded as a corporeal sort of thing like property or land.[1] Though they themselves dismiss

[1] (1923), II. 124-49.

this view, they still hold on to the assumption that the word denotes something which they say is an incorporeal thing. Bentham went one step further and, still assuming that the word 'right' denotes something, expressed the opinion that it denotes a fictitious object (entity).[2] In this he was followed by many nineteenth- and early twentieth-century jurists,[3] including Hohfeld.[4] A variation on this opinion was that of Hägerström,[5] the leader of the Scandinavian Realists, who held that the word 'right' referred to a mystical or supernatural power or bond, and a partial adherence to it was that of Hägerström's follower, Olivecrona, who sometimes, particularly in the first edition of his book, *Law as Fact*,[6] regarded a right as an object of one's imagination.[7] Later, however, Olivecrona, while agreeing with Bentham, Hägerström, and a long line of nineteenth-century writers that 'right' (like 'duty' etc.) does not denote 'anything real', more commonly took the more extreme view, foreshadowed by Hägerström,[8] that it does not denote at all. A later Scandinavian, Alf Ross, held, rather like those psychologists who replaced hypothetical constructs by intervening variables, that, for example, 'right' indicates only a functional correlation between certain conditioning facts and certain conditioned consequences.[9]

Clearly 'right' (like 'duty' etc.) does not denote any entity, whether physical, mental, or fictional. Having a right is neither like having a ring nor is it like having an idea. Nor is denying the existence of certain rights like denying the existence of centaurs or of El Dorado.

(b) 'Right' as fact-stating

Acceptance of the non-denoting function of 'right' etc. has, however, led many philosophers to the conclusion that

---

[2] (1945), 57-9; 71, n. 5; cp. (1970), 251-2. It may be that he meant that it was non-denotative.

[3] Cp. Olivecrona (1971), 163 ff.   [4] Hohfeld (1919), 30.

[5] (1953), 8, 16, 323.   [6] (1939), esp. ch. III.   [7] (1971), 184.

[8] e.g. (1953), 143; cp. 8, 16.   [9] (1958), s. 36.

sentences in which such words occur do not express truths or state facts. Thus, Hägerström confessed himself unable to 'determine the facts which correspond to these ideas' (p.1), while Olivecrona declared categorically that 'the notion [of *right*] does not correspond to the facts'. That the non-denotative function of 'right', 'duty', etc. was one of his reasons for drawing this conclusion comes out clearly in his objection[10] that Ross's attempt[11] to hold both that the word 'right' does not denote and yet that sentences containing it 'refer [*inter alia*] to purely factual circumstances' is inconsistent.

The answer to this is that neither the view that a word denotes a fiction—as do the words 'centaur' and 'abominable snowman'—nor the view that a word does not denote at all—as the words 'chance', 'average', 'if', or 'but'—provides a good reason for supposing that a sentence containing them cannot state a fact. Thus, to hold that the phrase 'the average man' does not denote anything does not commit one to holding that remarks about the average man, such as that he is 5ft. 8in. tall, is married, and drinks seventy-four pints of beer a year, cannot state facts. It is significant that Olivecrona attempts to reconcile his thesis that the sentence 'A has a right to X' does not state a fact with his feeling that it, at least 'ostensibly', 'indirectly', conveys some information and in some sense says something 'correct'—though not, he thinks, in the sense of 'true', which he confines to statements of fact—by putting forward the implausible suggestion that the information it does convey results from 'assumptions' which we can legitimately make because of the circumstances in which we hear it.[12]

A second reason underlying Hägerström's (for example pp. 8, 16, 323) and Olivecrona's (pp. 193–7) denial that sentences containing the words 'right' ('duty', 'power', etc.) can make statements of fact is their equation of facts with something in the *physical world*. It was precisely because

---

[10] (1971), 181–2.   [11] (1958), 174.
[12] (1971), 193–7; 259–67.

Hägerström related rights, duties, etc. to 'supernatural powers and bonds' in a supernatural world that he concluded that they, unlike the topics of scientific discourse, were not 'factual relations'. As we shall find that this distinction between kinds of facts and this assumption that facts are sorts of entities in the world underlie Dworkin's distinction between 'hard' and 'soft' facts, I shall leave the objections to it until I discuss Dworkin's thesis below.

A third reason for the Scandinavian Realists' denial that sentences containing such words as 'right' and 'duty' state facts—a reason typical also of the Logical Positivists' thesis about evaluative judgements in general—was the belief that the grammatically indicative form of such sentences misleads us into thinking that they express judgements, that is something which can be true or false, and state facts, whereas they are in Hägerström's view (pp. 135–43) 'expressive' or in Olivecrona's (pp. 187–93, 261) and Ross's (p. 9) 'directive'. It would take us too far afield and over too familiar ground to consider here all the pros and cons of such a view.[13] Suffice to say, first, that there is no inconsistency in holding both that the function of an utterance is, for example, to express one's feelings or to direct another's conduct and that what is said in making such an utterance is true or false and, therefore, states or fails to state a fact. For example, when I warn or advise you by stating that if you do that again, you will get into trouble. Secondly, the denial that sentences containing evaluative words, like 'right', 'duty', etc., can state facts usually rests on the assumption, disproved above, that to do so there would need to exist strange objects which such words as 'good', 'ought', 'right', and 'duty' could denote.

More recently H. L. A. Hart has argued that sentences containing legal words, such as 'right', 'duty', 'ownership', etc., as well as sentences imputing actions to people, as in 'He did it', are not, at least in their 'primary', 'principal', 'distinctive', 'fundamental' function, used to describe anything or to state any facts, but to ascribe or claim, for example, rights or

[13] Cp. White (1970), ch. 3, s. (b).

responsibility, to deduce legal conclusions, or to express decisions.[14] In his earlier work[15] he also held that such sentences do not say anything true or false, but in a later work[16] he seems often to allow that they do, though, nevertheless, still denying that they state any facts.

His reasons for these views are similar to those we have just discussed. First, he moves from the premiss that 'there is nothing which simply "corresponds" to legal words' to the conclusion that 'these do not have the straightforward connection with counterparts in the world of fact which most ordinary words have'.[17] To this we can give the same answer as we gave to the Scandinavian Realists, whom indeed Hart[18] quotes in his support, namely that it is illegitimate to conclude that because a single expression, such as 'right' or 'average man', does not refer, therefore a sentence containing it cannot state a fact. Hart also sometimes makes the Scandinavian mistake of supposing that facts are something to which single expressions ought to be able to refer.[19]

Secondly, like the Scandinavian Realists, Hart argues that because sentences containing legal terms are often used to ascribe, claim, confer, deduce, etc., therefore they cannot also state facts. Thus, he supposes that because 'A has a right to X' ascribes a right or 'A is guilty' gives a verdict, just as 'He is out' expresses a cricket umpire's decision, therefore none of these can say anything true or false. We saw, however, that there is no reason why such sentences should not do several jobs even at the same time, just as 'You'll not make much money as a philosopher' may both state and advise, even though as advice it cannot be true or false and as a statement it cannot be good or bad.[20]

With Hart, this second reason for denying that sentences containing legal words can state facts shades into a third. Just

---

[14] (1949) and (1954).   [15] (1949), 164, 166.
[16] (1954), 47-9, 52-3, 60.   [17] (1954), 38, 39 n. 2, 47, 48.
[18] (1954), 41 n. 7.
[19] (1954), 39 n. 2, 47, 48; cp. 58 where he, inconsistently, allows that individual legal words can be 'correlated with the facts'.
[20] Cp. (1949), 162, 164.

as he was persuaded by his cricket analogy that the only analyses of the meaning of, for example, 'He is out' alternative to his own are the clearly mistaken suggestions that the sentence means either 'The ball has struck the wicket' or 'The batsman must leave the crease', so he was convinced that the only analyses of the meaning of, for example, 'A has a right' or 'X has made a contract with Y' alternative to his own are the clearly mistaken reductions of it either to 'the statements of fact required for its truth', such as, in the former case, that a certain legal system exists or, in the latter, that 'the parties have signed a written agreement' or to the 'statement of the legal consequences of its being true', such as that the courts will behave in a certain way, as the American Realists held, or that 'Y is bound to do certain things under the agreement'.[21] To this, however, the answer is that Hart has mistaken the relation between the sentence containing the legal words and the sentence expressing what he calls 'the statement of fact required for its truth'.[22] The two sentences 'X has made a contract with Y' and 'The parties have signed a written agreement' or 'A has a right to V' and 'A is in a certain legal position in regard to Ving', like the two sentences 'A is out' and 'The ball has struck A's wicket' or— to take some examples not given by Hart—'A committed bigamy with B' and 'A married B' or 'A repeated himself' and 'A did so and so' or 'A checkmated B' and 'A moved his queen to KB4' or 'A passed his examination' and 'A got 40 per cent' refer to the same item in different ways— because the same item is of, at least, two different kinds— and, hence, give two different descriptions in sentences of different meanings of the same situation and, as we can also say, state two different facts. It can be a fact both that A signed an agreement and that A has a contract, both that A is in a certain position and that A has a right to V, both that A married B and that A committed bigamy, both that the ball struck A's wicket and that A is out, both that A moved

---

[21] (1954), 38, 43-4, 45 n. 18.
[22] Similarly A. Ross (1958), ss. 3, 35.

his queen to KB4 and that A checkmated B.[23] Because the event or situation described by 'p' in the circumstances amounts to, constitutes or is correctly judged to be, that described by 'q', then, if it is a fact that p, it is a fact that q. It is a mistake to argue, as Hart[24] does, that because saying 'q' is neither stating the fact that p nor making a logical inference from it, nor equating 'q' with 'p', therefore 'q' cannot state a fact as well as 'p'. Though the cricket statement that A is out is not identical with any of the statements of the various ways in which A can be out, for example by being bowled, stumped, or caught, and, therefore, does not state the same fact as is stated by the sentence stating any of them—though it may describe the same episode as one of them—it can state some fact.

If a certain form of words, for example the sentence 'p', says how things are, and if things are as the sentence 'p' says they are, then it is a fact that p. Furthermore, if things are as a particular sentence 'p' says they are, then not only is it a fact that p, but it is true to say that p. It is only because Hart does not keep in mind this latter connection that he can say, as he sometimes inconsistently does, both that such a sentence as 'A has made a contract with B' or 'A has a right to V', like 'A is out' or 'A has taken a trick in bridge', is true and yet does not state a fact.[25] The reason for his inconsistency, I think, is that his reference to the 'facts required for the truth of the sentence', for example that the two parties have signed an agreement or that the ball has struck the wicket, leads him to overlook the fact *stated* by the sentence, for example that the parties have a contract or that the batsman is out. The fact which is stated by the sentence 'A has committed bigamy' is not the fact that A has married or the fact that A has a wife still living, which may be required for the truth of the original sentence. One should not conclude, as Hart seems to do, that since 'A has a right' does not state those facts in virtue of which it is true to say it, it,

---

[23] *Pace* A. Ross (1958), 173. [24] (1949), 162; (1954), 42, 53.
[25] (1954), 47-9, 52-3, 60.

therefore, does not state a fact at all. To say that I have just
repeated myself does not state the facts in virtue of which
this is true, for example that for the second time I accused
Hart of confusing p and q, but it does nevertheless state
a fact. An incidental reason for Hart's attempt to admit
truth while denying facts may also be that which we saw led
to Olivecrona's introduction of the idea of 'assumptions',
for Hart too cannot help admitting that his allegedly non-
factual sentences 'carry some information' with them by
their 'reference to some justifying facts'.[26]

In contrast to the Scandinavian Realists and Hart, Ronald
Dworkin has more recently argued that sentences expressing
such legal remarks as 'A has a right to X', 'The contract
between A and B is valid', or 'A is guilty of Z' are true or
false and can state facts.[27] His thesis, however, rests on
a mistaken and unnecessary argument. This argument is
that 'there is something else in the world besides hard facts,
in virtue of which propositions of law might be true' (p. 77),
where 'hard facts' are defined as 'physical facts and facts
about behaviour (including the thoughts and attitudes) of
people' (p. 76) and other kinds of facts are exemplified by
so-called 'moral facts' and 'facts of narrative consistency'
(pp. 78–9). Note that this differentiation is made in terms of
'part of the world'. Thus, Dworkin agrees with his opponents
that 'facts about narrative consistency are [not] part of the
external world in the same sense in which facts about the
weight of iron are part of the world' (p. 81); a point which
significantly he repeats in his next sentence as 'narrative
consistency is [not] . . . part of the external world in anything like the way that the weight of iron is'. What Dworkin's
argument does is to assume that facts are particular kinds of
parts of the world in the way that what they are about are
parts of the world; that is, he assimilates a fact about narrative consistency to narrative consistency itself and a fact

[26] (1949), 164.
[27] e.g. (1977b), esp. 76–81; cp. (1977a), chs. 4 and 13. Page references in the
text are to the former.

about the weight of iron to the weight of iron itself. This assimilation makes it easier to suppose that just as there are different kinds of furniture in the world, so there are different kinds of facts about the furniture of the world. Dworkin is led to posit debatable kinds of fact, his so-called 'hard' and 'non-hard' facts, his 'physical' and 'narrative consistency' facts, for exactly the same sorts of reasons as Bertrand Russell was led to populate the world with 'negative', 'universal', 'conditional' facts and other philosophers to populate it with 'moral' facts. Indeed, we saw that the Scandinavian Realists failed also to distinguish clearly between facts and items in the world to which some words and verbal expressions might refer.

But, despite what many famous philosophers, such as Moore, Russell, Austin, Wittgenstein, have said, facts are not, and do not have the characteristics of, any part of the world.[28] Unlike entities, objects, events, situations, or states of affairs, facts have no date or location. Unlike objects, facts cannot be created or destroyed, pointed to or avoided. Unlike events, facts are not something we can be overtaken by, involved in, or predict. Unlike situations, they are not something we can find ourselves in, be rescued from, or which can be transformed; they cannot be nasty, serious, or ticklish. Unlike states of affairs, facts do not begin, last, or end. Although there are innumerable facts, unlike situations or states of affairs, facts do not exist. A distinction can be drawn between the occurrence of an event or the existence of a state of affairs and the fact that such an event occurred or that such a state of affairs exists. Contrariwise, facts, but not events, situations, or states of affairs, can be disputed, challenged, assumed, or proved. Facts can be stated, whereas events and situations are described. There may be facts about an event, situation, or state of affairs, but not the latter about a fact. It can be a fact that p, but not an event, situation, or state of affairs, that p. Facts, unlike events or situations, can be expressed by hypotheticals

[28] For references, see White (1970), 80 nn. 6 and 7.

and negatives. For example, it may be a fact, but it could not be an event, that if Hitler had invaded England in 1940, he would have won the war, or that Hitler did not win the war. Necessarily true statements, such as 'Either there is a train or there is not a train to Leeds at 10.00 a.m.', state facts, but do not describe a situation or state of affairs.

In order to show that it can be true to say that and be a fact that someone has a right to such and such, one no more needs to posit extra parts of, or items in, the world than one does when it is a fact, for example, that the angles of a Lobatchevskian triangle do not equal 180°, that such and such expenses are unnecessary for your work, that the batsman was out, that the master behaved selfishly or that the servant was careless. Facts are dependent on objects, events, situations, characteristics, etc. in the world in that unless these things were related in various, even conditional or possible, ways, it would not be a fact that so and so. But facts are not themselves items that exist in space and time. It makes no sense to ask when and where such a fact occurred, is occurring, or will occur. All that is meant by saying that it is a fact that so and so is that so and so is how things are. A factual statement tells us how things are in the world, no more and no less. Of course, if one wants to distinguish facts about different kinds of things or facts which are facts for different kinds of reasons by calling them, as some philosophers[29] have done, 'brute facts' or 'institutional facts' or even 'hard' and 'not-hard' facts, as Dworkin does, this is not objectionable in itself. What is objectionable is the assumption, first, that they are not both facts in exactly the same sense and, more so, that either are objects in the world.

(c) The locus of rights

If the notion of *a right* is not to be understood by seeking some item which it, or any word expressing it, denotes, let us turn for understanding it to the circumstances in which

[29] e.g. Anscombe (1958), 69–72; Searle (1969), ch. 2, s. 7.

it is used and to the relations it has to other notions which are commonly associated in thought with it. The circumstances of its use include the possible objects of rights, the possible subjects, and the possible grounds. The associated notions include *right* itself, *ought, obligation, duty, liberty, privilege, power*, and *claim.*

A consideration of these will set us several tasks. First, we need to discover what are the possible objects of rights. That is, to answer the question 'What can there be a right *to*?' We shall see that inadequate theories of rights can arise because account is taken only of rights to receive or only of these and of rights to act, whereas there can also be rights to be in a certain state, to feel certain things, and to have or take certain attitudes. Secondly, we need to examine possible holders of a right. That is, to answer the question 'Who or what can have a right?' Are rights, strictly speaking, confined to adult human beings or can children, babies, foetuses, the mentally handicapped, generations yet unborn, animals, and even inanimate nature have rights? Thirdly, we need to assess various suggested grounds of rights, since, as we shall see, a basic characteristic of the notion of a right is the appropriateness of the question 'What gives you the right to . . .?' Fourthly, we need to chart the relevant positions of the notion of *a right* and of the various notions—such as *right, ought, obligation, duty, privilege, power*, and *claim*—with which it is commonly accompanied and with many of which it is frequently assimilated or confused. Here we need to avoid both the Hohfeldian assumption that 'a right' is an ambiguous term used to cover such notions as liberty, power, and claim and the more recent suggestion that it refers to a complex structure of some or all of these.[30]

---

[30] Wellman (1982), ch. I.

2

The Variety of Rights

(a) *Extent of rights*

Rights can be grouped in various ways. They may be grouped, for example, according to what they are rights to, according to whose rights they are, according to what class they belong to, or according to whether they are specific or general.

i.

One's right may be a right *to do* something, such as to worship as one pleases or to pursue one's trade freely. These are sometimes called 'active' rights. Or it may be a right *to have something done* to one, such as to be looked after in one's old age or to be told the truth by one's doctor. These are sometimes called 'passive' or 'recipient' rights. Or it may be a right *to be in a certain state*, such as to be free or happy. Or a right *to feel* something, such as to feel annoyed, disappointed, pleased, or proud. Or a right *to take a certain attitude*, such as to assume that p, to expect that q, or to hope that r. Rights *to* or *of* something embrace all of these; for example a right to education or a living wage, to free speech or privacy, to happiness or to a particular assumption, to trial by one's peers or consideration by one's children, as well as a right of way, of search, or of appeal.

It is important not to confine one's examination or one's theories of rights only to the first two species, that is to rights to do so and so or to have such and such done to one. Such a one-sided diet of examples is, for instance, a root cause of the common mistakes that every right implies a claim and that it implies a duty, for example a claim that others not interfere with what one wants to do or that others provide what one wants to have done to one and the duty of others either not to interfere or to provide. It also gives undue plausibility to an analysis of a right as what justifies interference with another's freedom.[1] It may, further, be the source of the view that rights can only be social;[2] that, for example, one person's right is necessarily founded on another person's behaviour.[3]

There are admittedly all sorts of relations between the rights of one person and the duties, obligations, privileges, powers, etc. which another has and what it is right or wrong for him to do and what he ought to do. So that often if someone has a right to do so and so, what he does will be right and it will be wrong for others to interfere or even a duty on others to help. But these relations depend very much on the circumstances of the case. That they do not always hold becomes clear when further examples are taken. And the reason why they do not always hold is, as I shall be arguing, that these relations are not purely conceptual, that is, not purely dependent on the nature of the concepts of *right, wrong, ought*, etc. Thus, even if Robinson Crusoe could not have had any legal or, perhaps, moral rights, he certainly could have had the right to feel pleased or proud, to assume that p, to hope that q, or to expect that r, for these rights do not relate to what others do. Indeed, even when others are involved, my right, for example to pursue my business interests, need not make it wrong for them to interfere nor need it lay on them any duty to help. This is not to forget that, of course, anyone who has a right will, because of his right, be immune from, or have a basis for justifying himself against, at least certain sorts of criticism for the things he does, even when these are things which he would be properly criticized for doing in other circumstances or others would be properly criticized for doing even in these circumstances and, furthermore, properly criticized

[1] e.g. Hart (1955).
[2] e.g. Golding (1968); Plamenatz (1950); Henle (1980), 89; Levine (1980), 137.   [3] Dias (1970), 241.

on grounds which would seem prima facie applicable to the things he does within his rights. Moreover, these others would often be criticizable for interfering or even for not helping with what he did, where such interference or help is appropriate.

A one-sided concentration on the so-called 'passive rights' has led some[4] to suppose that only these are rights and that the so-called 'active' rights are really only liberties, while a one-sided concentration on 'active' rights has led others[5] to insist that every right must be exercisable, which 'passive' rights are not. The former myopia explicitly rules out any right of self-defence, of combination, or of way, while the latter automatically precludes the attribution of rights to animals, inanimate nature, and even babies.

There are, on the other hand, things which it makes no sense to talk of one's having a right to or, indeed, of their being right. One cannot have a right, nor can it be right (or wrong), to succeed or fail, perceive or remember, to ache or itch, to imagine or dream, to bleed or tremble. For none of these is in the power either of the agent or of another.

In addition to the division of rights into these logically different kinds of thing to which one can have them, there are innumerable different ways of materially grouping the objects of rights. For instance, Salmond included rights regarding oneself, one's domestic relations, one's property, one's reputation etc.[6]

ii.

Rights are frequently grouped by the type of holder of the right, such as human or animal rights, parental or children's rights, citizen's or soldier's rights, buyer's or seller's rights, etc., since it is in virtue of being such a type of holder that one has the particular rights. Depending on the type of

---

[4] e.g. Williams (1956); Raphael (1965).
[5] e.g. McCloskey (1979), 28, 31.
[6] (1947), 76.

holder such rights may be to do or receive, to feel or to be, etc.

iii.

A host of concepts, such as right, ought, obliged, necessary, principle, rule, law, etc., have application in various fields, differentiated from each other by the system of operations which holds in each. Principles, rules, and laws can be moral, legal, logical, conventional, etc., and something can be morally, legally, logically, etc., right or necessary, or what one is obliged or ought to do. Similarly, with *rights*. Rights can be distinguished as moral or legal, religious or political, statutory, constitutional, customary or conventional, epistemological or logical, etc. Thus, one may have a moral, but not a legal, right to oppose a certain measure; a statutory right to a state pension, a customary right to a certain place at table, or a constitutional right to vote in the club elections. Someone's right to assume so and so or to conclude such and such in an argument could, perhaps, be called logical; while a visitor's right to expect to be treated courteously may be conventional. Many rights, which have their origin in the particular circumstances of the case, such as a right to criticize or to complain, to smile or to express surprise, to feel disappointed or pleased, to hope or to expect are not usually or necessarily classified as either moral or logical, constitutional or conventional.

Whether so and so is a moral, a legal, a logical, or some other kind of right will relate to its origin and to the kind of grounds on which it is based and justified. It may be, for example, because of a moral or legal code or the rules of logic or because of one's previous or present circumstances and position that one has a right to V. There is no reason why the same thing, for example to vote in a club election, cannot be something to which one has various kinds of right, for example, legal, moral, and conventional.

iv.

A right may be general, rather than restricted, because of how widely it is possessed. Or it may be general, rather than specific, because it is a right to something of a general kind, such as a right to education, to vote, to drive a car. Such general rights are usually based on some characteristics of or some general rules about classes of holders, whether human beings, citizens, or those over seventeen. Specific rights may be either particular instances of such rights, as a right to drive this car or to vote in this election, or rights which arise out of particular circumstances, such as my right to criticize your performance, to be disappointed at my reception, or to hope for a change.

(b) Characteristics of rights

A right as such is something one can have or be given, earn, enjoy, or exercise. It is something one can claim, demand, assert, insist on, fight for, or secure or what one can waive, surrender, relinquish, or forfeit. It can be recognized and protected or disregarded, altered, abridged, infringed, whittled away, violated, or trampled on. Rights to particular kinds of things, however, may lack various of these qualities because of the differences in what they are rights to. Thus, whereas any right can be had or claimed, asserted or denied, allowed or disregarded, only a right to do so and so and not a right to receive such and such can be exercised, since only what one does oneself is in one's power or control. One can exercise one's right to vote, but not to be fed.

One's right to receive will call for assistance from others and involve—though not, I shall argue, logically imply—obligations, duties, and claims on them to help; whereas one's rights to act will call for protection and involve obligations and duties on others not to interfere. Because my right to do things is linked to my doing something, it is I who in this area will be immune from or open to criticism, who will be acting within or not within my rights; whereas because my right to have things done to or for me is linked to other people's doing something, it is in this area they who will be open to or immune from criticism, who will be infringing or not infringing my rights or failing or not failing to do their duty.

It is because to feel so and so, whether disappointed or pleased, and to have a certain attitude, whether to assume, to expect or to hope, are not under the control or in the gift of another, that no question arises of being given, demanding, insisting on, fighting for, or securing, a right to these, nor of the right to these being violated or trampled on, nor its exercise prevented. The irrelevance of another's control over one's feelings and attitudes precludes also both the idea of a claim on another and the idea of a duty of another either to refrain from interference or to give positive help when what one has a right to is, for example, to feel indignant at such and such or to hope for so and so.

Finally, though one can alter, abridge, or whittle away a general right, such as the right to free speech or to education, there is often no room in a specific right, such as the right to criticize a particular performance or to be present on a particular occasion, for such alteration. One expects charters and bills of rights to contain general, not specific, rights. One classes one's right to free speech, to education, to vote, or to be fed, but not one's right to assume p, feel proud of x, complain about y, as 'one of one's rights'.

Similarly, the differences between moral and legal rights are also due to the characteristics of the areas in which they are rights. The question, for example, whether a divorced man has a legal or only a moral right to access to his children in their mother's care does not depend on any difference in the notion of a right, but on the different kinds of grounds and origin of a moral and a legal right. Nor does the supposition that the meaning of 'right' (or 'duty' or 'obligation') in moral and legal contexts is the same commit one to holding that legal and moral rights (or duties or obligations) are necessarily related.[7]

The differences between rights which can be exercised and those which cannot, between those which can be violated or interfered with and those which cannot, or between those which are rights to do and rights to receive, rights to be and rights to feel, as well as the differences between those which are legal and those which are moral, no more depend on different notions of right, or different senses of 'right' or even different kinds of rights, than the differences between what is good in itself and what is good for something else, between what is logically and what is practically necessary or between what is morally and what is legally obliged depend on different notions of *good, necessity,* or *obligation.* All such differences depend on differences in the qualifying characteristics, not on any differences in what is qualified.[8]

[7] *Pace* Hart (1982), 145–61, esp. 145, 147.   [8] Cp. White (1971).

3

Duty

The most frequent attempts, by both philosophers and jurisprudents, to explain the notion of a right utilize the notion either of a duty or, what is often assimilated to it, the notion of an obligation. So that duties (or obligations), for example, are said to be correlative with or a ground of a right or are used as a distinguishing mark either between rights and privileges or between rights and liberties. Bentham and others, indeed, argued that since, in their view, rights and duties are correlative, the idea of a right could be regarded as superfluous and all the necessary work be done by the idea of duty. Historically, the notion of a *duty* seems as old as the Stoic τὸ καθῆκον, which Cicero and the Roman jurists translated as 'officium', whereas the idea of *a right*—what the French jurists call 'droit subjectif' and the Germans 'subjective Recht'—as contrasted merely with *right* or *law*, may not strictly be older than the Middle Ages.[1]

I shall argue in Chapter 5 against these alleged logical links between rights and either duties or obligations—which latter I shall also argue are different from each other. A necessary preliminary is an examination of the notions of a *duty* and of an *obligation* and, incidentally, of the notion of *ought*, to which duty and obligation are also commonly assimilated. This examination will occupy this and the next chapter.

(a) Duties and jobs

A duty, as its etymology suggests, is something which is due, something which falls to be done, either because it is simply assigned or because it is involved in, prescribed by, part and

[1] Cp. Villey (1962), esp. ch. XI, who suggests Ockham in the fourteenth century; Pound (1959), IV. 60 gives Donellus, *De Jure Civili* 3. 2–4 (1589).

parcel of, arises out of, or owes its existence to, a particular
institutionalized position. Duties are commonly attached to
roles or jobs. Indeed, the Latin for 'duty' is 'officium', that
is, office; and the OED defines an 'office' as a position with
duties attached to it. They are usually the duties *of* the
holders of these roles or jobs. 'In my station', as Bradley
said, 'my particular duties are prescribed to me.' It is as
a teacher, policeman, or magistrate that I have certain duties.
There are professional, military, and domestic duties. If
I apply for a job I want to know what its duties are. Are
they many or few, time-consuming or light? My duties may
be legally or quasi-legally defined, or they may be implicit
in the kind of position I hold. A contract of service makes
clear the duties of a university teacher, a student society may
draw up a list of duties of its secretary, while the duties of
a parent can only be assessed from a knowledge of the
position of a parent in society. When the duties attached to
a job or position change markedly, then the job or position
is no longer what it was. If a schoolteacher's duties are
extended to include helping children to dress and to feed
themselves and looking after their health, he may rightly
complain that he is being asked to be a nanny and a nurse.
Different societies expect different duties from parents
because they regard the position of parenthood differently.
A position, and therefore its duties, may be defined partly
by the law of the land and partly in professional and trade
codes. The Hippocratic oath, the General Medical Council,
and the law all have an influence in the specification of the
duties of a doctor. What constitutes a proper parent or a con-
scientious citizen depends not merely on legal definitions,
but partly on the mores of society and partly on the conscience of the individual. Besides his legal duties, a parent or
citizen has, therefore, moral duties; that is, work to be done
according to the dictates of his society or himself. The
question 'What is my duty?' depends for its answer partly on
what view I take of my position. The more I regard my
position in a moral as well as a legal or professional light, the

more I will see in it moral as well as legal duties. When in England it was the legal duty only of the mother to support an illegitimate child, some fathers may have considered it to be their moral duty. In a leading case, it was held that in certain circumstances there was a moral and social duty, but no legal duty, to help the police.[2]

When I take on a job I take on certain duties. I can go or be on or off duty; I can report for duty. A policeman can be on point duty and a nurse on night duty. I may even be able to stand duty for someone else. My duties commence and finish with my work. The day I take up my job is the day I take up my duties. Specific tasks can be explained as being the duty of the president or of the secretary, of the police or the fire department. We can excuse our own non-performance by protesting that it was not our duty or our job to do it, but that of someone else. A man is not doing his job properly if he does not carry out his duties; certain duties are expected of us because of our position. If someone tells me or reminds me of my duties, he tells or reminds me what I have to do as part of the job. He can impose a duty on me or I can make it my duty to do so and so. I can do, perform, or carry out my duty or I can try to do it. I can neglect it, shirk it, fail in it, or be unable to do it or be hindered in the execution of it. I can be guilty of a dereliction, neglect, or breach of duty. I can be relieved of my duties. I may explain my action by pleading that I have my duty to do and that I was only doing it. I may feel that something is my duty; a sense of duty may make me do it. Sometimes I answer the call of duty; sometimes what I do is beyond the call of duty. I may earn the title of a dutiful son or servant.

Many positions are permanent or semi-permanent. I don't have times on and off duty as a parent, a husband, or a citizen. There are certain things which, as a parent or a citizen, I must always be prepared to do. Bradley went so far as to say that 'the only way to do your duty is to do your duties'.[3] Because I occupy different positions and have several different

[2] *Rice* v. *Connolly* [1966], 2 QB 414.   [3] (1876), 152.

jobs at the same time, I can have conflicting duties.[4] My duties as a teacher may conflict with those as a parent, those as a doctor with those as a husband. Though the law will naturally try to avoid conflicts in the duties it assigns, this is not always possible,[5] as when a bus driver has a duty both to drive with due care and attention and yet to adhere to a time schedule.[6]

The close connection between a duty and a job, role, or position explains also the restriction of duties to certain sorts of subjects. It is because they are capable of undertaking jobs that normal people are the usual subjects of duties. Similarly, because the state and the local authority occupy a certain position and have certain functions, they also have duties, for example not to discriminate against the goods of certain foreign states or to secure accommodation for the homeless. In a collection of states, such as the European community, each state is credited with various duties and rights, not only in regard to its own citizens, but also *vis-à-vis* each other.[7] On the other hand, inanimate objects, whether natural or man made, clearly cannot have duties either to do something or to somebody. Nor can such undeveloped animate objects as foetuses or babies. Even staunch defenders of the rights of animals usually admit that they cannot have duties;[8] though, interestingly, the link between the ideas of a duty and a job is preserved, both for animals and the inanimate in, perhaps metaphorical, talk of a dog being on guard duty or of a battery being of heavy-duty standard. Whether these can be literally the subjects of duties depends on whether it makes sense to talk of them undertaking, carrying out, doing, shirking, or failing in their duties or their duty, or of being assigned or relieved of their duties. Whether or not a dog can have a duty, for example to its master, a battery clearly cannot.

[4] Cp. Bradley (1876), 156–7.
[5] e.g. *Sheriff of Middlesex* (1840) ii Ad. and El. 273.
[6] e.g. *Daly* v. *Liverpool Corporation* [1939] 2 All ER 142.
[7] Cp. Lasok (1980).
[8] e.g. Feinberg (1976), 191–2; (1978), 49; Brandt (1959), 440.

Though sanctions are frequently attached to breaches of duty, so that one who fails in his duty may be sacked from his job, morally disapproved of, or legally proceeded against, this is not invariably, much less necessarily, so. It is, therefore, no part of the notion of a duty as such.[9] The law in fact allows the existence of 'unenforcable duties',[10] the impossibility of applying a sanction in some cases of breach of duty, for example where the offender is covered by diplomatic privilege[11] or has died, and even the idea of a 'sanctionless duty'.[12] As Cotton LJ said, 'Statute-barred debts are due, though payment of them cannot be enforced by action.'[13] An 'immunity from suit' is not an 'immunity from duty'.[14] Hence, it is a mistake to define a 'duty' as a 'contingent liability to a sanction'.[15]

The link between duties and jobs, roles or positions depends on the idea of a duty being something due or assigned. Thus, while plumbers, sailors, tennis players, and brothers have roles just as much as doctors, teachers, umpires, and parents, duties seem to go more automatically with the latter roles because the role includes much that is morally, legally, or otherwise due from it. It has an institutionalized place.

Moral duty may have entered ethics from religion, where it finds a natural place as that which is due from a person to his God or which his God lays on him as a servant or creature of his. Later it became linked with the tasks which are morally required of one because of one's position, whether these are tasks which one simply has a duty to do, as in writing references to give an honest appraisal, or which are due to some particular persons, as from a parent to his

[9] *Pace* Austin (1861), I. 444; (1832), 14–18; Hart (1958), 95; Holmes (1897); Kelsen (1946), 63; Feinberg (1960), 278. Contrast Hart (1961), 34–5, 211–15, 244.

[10] *Kaye* v. *Sutherland* (1888) 20 QBD 147 at 151; *Tassell* v. *Hallen* [1892] I QB 321.

[11] For references to cases, see Dias (1970), 219–28.

[12] e.g. *Dickenson* v. *Del Solar* [1930] 1 KB 376 *per* Hewart LCJ at 380.

[13] *Cerwen* v. *Millburn* (1889) 42 Ch. D. 424 at 434.

[14] *Broom* v. *Morgan* [1953] 1 QB 597 *per* Denning LJ at 609–10.

[15] Quoted, but disagreed with, by Jenks (1933), ch. VIII.

children. Often, as we shall see, the idea of duty degenerated among moral philosophers into a mere synonym for 'ought'.

Legal duties may be either absolute, that is laid upon everyone, for example not to commit suicide or not to carry offensive weapons in public, or they may, as with duties of care, be characterized as those of certain classes of persons or of persons who put themselves in certain positions, for example the duty of a licensee or the manufacturer of proprietary medicines or the duty of persons who keep barrels in a warehouse.

Just as philosophers tend to assimilate what one ought to do to what it is right for one to do, so the law itself and jurisprudents tend to regard anything which the law, either by Act of Parliament or in the common law, requires us to do or refrain from, especially if stated in a rule, as a duty and any commission of a legally wrong act as a breach of a duty.[16] Duty becomes associated more with something we are assigned to do than with something due from our job.

Sometimes an Act will speak only of what so and so 'shall', 'should', or 'must' do, but sometimes it explicitly mentions a duty to do so and so.[17] The general jurisprudential thesis that what the law requires or prohibits is a duty is used by Hart to characterize what he calls the 'primary rules' of a legal system.[18]

(b) A duty to do something and a duty to someone

A duty is always a duty *to do* so and so or a duty *to* such and such. Duties *to do* so and so include duties *to act*, for example to chair a meeting, to clothe one's children, or to keep records; or *to forbear* from acting, for example not to interfere, not to carry offensive weapons; or *to achieve*, for example to ensure that nothing is lost, to find a replacement, or to arrive early; or, perhaps, *to be*, for example impartial,

---

[16] e.g. Salmond (1947), ss. 73–4.
[17] e.g. The Merchant Shipping Act 1894 s. 422(1); Children and Young Persons Act 1969, s. 2(1).   [18] (1961).

helpful, or vigilant. But there are no duties *to have* something *done* to one—as distinct from a duty to allow, submit to, or undergo this—*to feel* so and so or *to have* an attitude of some sort. Duties *to* such and such include duties to persons, perhaps even to the dead, as well as to personified institutions, such as one's university or one's country, and even to one's science or one's art. There are, however, no duties to inanimate things, such as trees or buildings. Philosophers dispute whether one can have a duty to oneself. Kant, for instance, regarded the negative duties not to commit suicide or to indulge in drink, drugs, gluttony, unnatural sex, cruelty to animals, or wanton destruction of nature, and the positive duties to cultivate physical, intellectual, and moral perfection, as duties to oneself, while Paley took the same view of the duties of not committing suicide or getting drunk.[19]

Others, such as Hart, Whiteley, and M. G. Singer, have denied the possibility of a duty to oneself.[20] Further, some such as Aquinas, Kant, Ritchie, and Rickaby, have denied that we can have duties to animals, whereas others, such as Feinberg, Regan, and Rachels, insist that we can.[21]

A duty to do so and so often involves a duty to such and such. Thus, much of what a chairman of a company has a duty to do is a duty to his shareholders as many of a doctor's duties are to his patients, of a parent to his children, of a citizen to his country, of an actor to his art and his public. The duty of looking after her widowed father may be a duty which a daughter owes to him.

But not all duties *to do* something involve a duty *to* anything. The duty of a judge to pass sentence is not owed to anyone. It may be the company chairman's duty to his shareholders to refuse a take-over bid, but his duty to chair

---

[19] Kant, *Metaphysische Anfangsgründe der Tugendlehre* (1797); Paley, *Moral and Political Philosophy* (1785), Bk. IV; cp. Bentham (1789), ch. XVII. 6; Hill (1973), s. V.

[20] Hart (1958), 180; Whiteley (1953); M. G. Singer (1959); contrast Wick (1960).

[21] See references in Singer and Regan (1976) and compare Feinberg (1978). Whiteley (1953) also denies duties to animals.

meetings is not a duty to anyone. A doctor's duty to his patient includes a refusal to reveal to a third party anything told to him in confidence, but his duty, imposed by the Ministry of Health, to keep a record of all consultations is not a duty to anyone. The person to whom one is answerable for any neglect of one's duties is not necessarily the person to whom a particular one of those duties is owed. A doctor owes it to his patient to tell him the truth about his illness, but it is the Ministry of Health who will hold him responsible for such a failure of duty. In the law, the so-called 'absolute duties', for example not to carry offensive weapons in public, to insure one's car, or to observe road signs, are not duties to anyone.[22]

Even where what one has a duty to do is to treat someone in a certain way or to do something for him, or even where one has a duty towards or in regard to him, it does not follow that one has a duty *to* him.[23] Neither one's duty to sentence the prisoner nor to stop the burglar is a duty to him. It may be part of a daughter's duty to her widowed father to entertain his friends, but though his friends are the beneficiaries of her duty, she does not owe it to them. This is even clearer when what we have a duty to do something *for* either certainly or debatably cannot be something we could have a duty *to*. One could have a duty to do something for the preservation of Venice or the protection of birds without its being a duty to them. Nor could one's duty to polish the silver or change the oil filter be a duty to them. Hence, to admit that we have a duty to do something in regard to, or even for, animals does not imply that we have a duty to them. Equally, the examples given by Kant and others of duties regarding ourselves, such as not neglecting our talents or committing suicide, can be understood without supposing that they have to be duties to ourselves.

[22] Contrast *East Suffolk Rivers Catchment Board* v. *Kent* [1941] AC 74 *per* Lord Atkin at 88, 'a duty conferred by statute is primarily a duty owed to the state'.
[23] *Pace* many of the writers in Bridge *et al.* (1973) who pass easily from 'a duty to V for X' to 'a duty to X'; cp. Narveson (1978), 43, 45, who says a duty to do something implies a duty to someone.

In fact, a duty to such and such involves a duty to do so and so, but not conversely.

(c) Duty *and* ought

Despite what philosophers[24] and jurisprudents[25] commonly say, the notions of *duty* and *ought*, and of what we have a duty to do and what we ought to do, are quite different. A duty, as its etymology suggests, is something which is due from whoever has the duty. It is, as we have seen, due either because of the institutionalized position one has, the class of person one is, the nature of the job one has undertaken or had allocated to one, the laws of the land, or the regulations of a group or a moral code. What ought to be done, on the other hand, is what it is appropriate, fitting, or 'owing' in the circumstances to do. Unlike a duty, what ought to be done might, and often does, follow from the characteristics or consequences of the proposed deed. Perhaps I ought to do so and so because it is an act of mercy or charity or because it will have the best results. But this is not what makes it my duty; that is, something due from me because laid on me or owing from my legal or moral position. It may well be that I ought to feed a starving beggar, but I do not have a duty to feed him in the way that I have a duty to feed my starving children or servants, unless you insist, for example, that it is my 'Christian duty', that is, my duty as a Christian. Even some of the things which I ought to do in virtue of my particular position are no part of the duties of that position. It is because what I ought to do is linked to what is the appropriate thing in the circumstances that I can give advice by saying what ought to be done. By contrast, to tell someone what his duty is is not to advise, but to inform and insist.

The relations between what one ought to do and what one has a duty to do are similar to those between what ought

---

[24] e.g. Prichard (1940), 86 ff.; Ross (1930); cp. Hobbes, *Leviathan*, ch. 14; contrast Whiteley (1953).

[25] e.g. Dias (1970), 204; Smith (1976), ch. III.

to happen and what is due to happen. Though it may be that the tyres on my car both ought to be renewed and are due for renewal, the latter can only be because of some rule about the time between changes, whereas the former may be either for this reason or some other, such as the amount of wear on their treads. To say that the bus ought to have arrived before now is not the same as saying that it is now overdue. Just as I often ought to do things which I have no duty to do, so things often ought to be done and ought to happen which are not due to be done or to happen. That something is my duty is a reason why I ought to do it, just as the fact that something is due to happen is a reason why it ought to happen. It is not, however, necessarily a sufficient reason. Sometimes I ought not to do what it is my duty to do just as it is sometimes true that what is due to happen ought nevertheless not to happen. On the other hand, the mere fact that I ought to do so and so gives me no reason for supposing that it is my duty to do it any more than the mere fact that something ought to happen is a reason for supposing that it is due to happen.

Further, whatever the truth in the dictum that 'ought' implies 'can', it is clear that I often cannot do my duty. Similarly, whatever the force of the legal dictum that 'Lex non cogit ad impossibilia', the inability to have done otherwise is no excuse for a breach of any 'strict' duty.

On the other hand, whereas the idea of *ought* can go with almost anything, whether it be a deed, a happening, an achievement, a result, a feeling, a state, etc., the idea of *duty* is confined to what one can *do*. It makes sense to say, for example, that someone ought to be killed, to become so and so, or to achieve such and such, to feel ashamed of this, to be dissatisfied with that or content with the other; but these can hardly be one's duties.

Nor can a conflict of duties be resolved by subsuming them under one wider duty in the way that, perhaps, the question whether I ought to do one thing or another has in theory an answer.

It is significant that the law, where the notion of duty looms large, does not make much use of the notion of *ought*. This is because when I am bidden to do so and so or forbidden to do such and such by the law, it is illegal to disobey not because of the nature of the bidden or forbidden act, but because there is a legal rule, whether laid down by statute or arising from the common law, about it. Thus, cruelty to animals is something which morally I ought not to indulge in because of the kind of thing it is, but which I have a legal duty to forbear from because of an Act of Parliament.

An indication that the notion of *ought* is separate from that of *duty* is the fact that though when what is at issue is what someone ought *to do*, the notion of ought is more plausibly linked with what one has a duty to do, when what is at issue is what one ought *to receive*, the notion is more plausibly linked with what one has a right to receive. This is why it has commonly, though still mistakenly, been held that what we ought to do we have a duty to do and that what we ought to be given we have a right to be given, and vice versa. But no one, I think, has argued that we necessarily ought to do what we have a right to do or that we ought to be given what, it hardly makes sense to say, we have a duty to be given, or vice versa.

(d) Duty *and* obligation

The other important notion which that of a duty is commonly assimilated to is that of *obligation*. Thus, philosophers[26] and jurisprudents[27] either treat the two similarly, often sliding to and fro in their discussions from one to the other, or explicitly equate them. Bentham spoke of '*duties*, or what is another

---

[26] e.g. Kant; Nowell-Smith (1954), 200; Lamont (1946); Brandt (1958), 34-8; Whiteley (1953).

[27] e.g. Salmond (1957), chs. 10 and 11; Austin (1832), 14-18; Whateley, Jenks, Olivecrona; Smith (1976), 44 *et passim*; and many contributors to *Fundamental Duties*, Bridge (1973), e.g. pp. 34, 55, 81, 86, 144, 204, 219, 249, 253, etc.

name for the same thing, *obligations*'.[28] And Hart admits that though there is a difference, they are usually treated similarly in the law.[29] The actual cases often either use them indifferently[30] or explicitly make them synonymous.[31]

In order to see more clearly the differences—and the similarities—between the two notions, both of which have been used in exactly the same way to explicate the idea of a right, it is worth first examining the notion of an obligation, and that of being obliged, on its own.

[28] (1970), 294.

[29] (1961), 238 n. In (1958) he uses them indifferently.

[30] e.g. *Rylands* v. *Fletcher* (1868) LR 3 HL 330; *Australasian Steam Navigation Co.* v. *Morse* (1872) 8 Moore NS 482; *Rice* v. *Connolly* [1966] 2 QB 414 *per* Parker LJ at 419.

[31] e.g. *The San Onofre* [1922] All ER 720 *per* Atkin LJ at 724.

4

Obligation

Wherever the notion of *obligation* is operative, the notion of *being obliged* is also operative, though not vice versa. For this reason, it is important to understand the notion of *being obliged* and its relation to that of *obligation*. Furthermore, an influential contemporary jurisprudential thesis, that of H. L. A. Hart, is partly based on a particular interpretation of the difference between the two.

(a) 'Obliged by' and 'obliged to'

If I am obliged by somebody or something to do X, then he or it obliges me to do X. If, on the other hand, I am obliged to somebody, or perhaps something, for doing Y (or for Z), then he or it obliges me by doing Y (or with Z). For instance, in the first case, if I am obliged by the Vice-Chancellor, a university regulation or the illness of a colleague, to attend a meeting, then the Vice-Chancellor, a university regulation, or the illness of a colleague, obliges me to attend a meeting. In the second case, if I am obliged to the desk clerk for (or for giving me) the required information, then he obliges me with (or by giving me) the required information.

I am not obliged *to* what I am obliged *by*, nor obliged *by* what I am obliged *to*. The person, or thing, to whom I am obliged has helped me; the person, or thing, by whom I am obliged has not. The person to whom I am obliged is obliging, but not the person by whom I am obliged. An obliging person is necessarily helpful. I am obliged to someone for his doing of something, but obliged by someone only by his doing of something. I am obliged to someone because of what he has done for me, but obliged by him because of what he has done to me. I can be obliged to someone to a greater or lesser degree, but there are no degrees to which I can be obliged by someone. I can either be obliged to someone or be obliged by someone to do something, but I cannot be obliged to someone to do something nor can I be obliged by someone without being obliged by him to do something.

The one is, however, basically similar to the other. Whether I am obliged to someone for what he has done or obliged by him by what he has done, whether he simply obliges me or obliges me to do something, I am obliged by his doing of something. Further, though I cannot be obliged to myself for what I myself do, I can be obliged to do so and so by what I myself do, as when I am obliged to do X by my having promised or contracted to do it. Finally, when what obliges me to do something is not a person at all, but, for example, a rule or a physical event or a psychological condition, then also there is something by which, though nothing to which, I am obliged. In every case of being obliged, therefore, whether I be obliged to someone or to do something, there is something, though not necessarily someone, by which I am obliged. That by which I am obliged may be called the 'obliging factor'.

Besides being obliged to or by, I can also feel obliged to or by someone or something or feel obliged to do so and so, irrespective of whether or not I am in fact obliged.

(b) 'Being obliged' and 'having an obligation'

I may have (or be under) an obligation to someone or to do something. An obligation may be assumed because of what I do, as when I make a promise, or incurred because of what someone has done for me, as when he helps me, or imposed because of what someone or something does to me, as when the law puts me under an obligation. I may acknowledge, fulfil, or be released from such an obligation. I may enter into negotiations with or without obligation. I may receive something which carries or is free from obligation.

To have (or be under) an obligation is normally to be

obliged. I am obliged to the person to whom I am under an obligation and obliged to do what I am under an obligation to do. I may, however, have an obligation or obligations— though I cannot be under an obligation—to someone according to which I am obliged to do something for him, though I am not obliged to him. Of this kind are treaty obligations, for example to come to the help of an ally in the event of an attack by a third power, or family obligations, for example to play with my children; or a doctor's obligations to his patients. I have obligations to my allies, my children, and my patients, and am, therefore, obliged to do something for them; though I am not obliged to them, nor under an obligation to them. Further, I can have some obligation, but not be somewhat obliged, to do so and so; and I can have various obligations, for example to my students, without being obliged to do something specific.

But though to have (or be under) an obligation is normally to be obliged, the converse is not true. I am often obliged without having (or being under) an obligation. Neither the yachtsman who is obliged by the wind to alter course, nor the traveller who is obliged by the gunman to hand over his wallet, nor the candidate who is obliged to take paper X, nor the chess player who is obliged to sacrifice his bishop, has (or is under) an obligation to do what he is obliged to do. Animals can be obliged, for example by circumstances, to do so and so, but cannot have obligations. I may even feel morally obliged, for example, to allow a student to miss lectures because of the sudden illness of his mother, without feeling I have, or am under, an obligation to do so.

Having (or being under) an obligation, like having or being under orders, having a requirement or being under suspicion, has an additional implication of a continuous state of which 'obliged', 'ordered', 'required', and 'suspected' are free. Hence, 'having (or being under) an obligation' is usually confined to contexts where there is a systematic pattern of rules, regulations, principles, relationships, etc., which bind one in various ways in various circumstances as contrasted with being bound merely by force of circumstances.[1] Thus, there are legal and moral, political and social, religious and family obligations, but not physical or psychological obligations, though one can be obliged either legally, morally, politically, and socially, or by family relationships and religious affiliations, or by physical and psychological circumstances.

The fact that the notion of *obligation* is different from that of *being obliged* and that the former is confined to certain contexts, such as the legal and the moral, does not, however, show that the notion of being obliged in 'legally or morally obliged' is different from that in 'obliged by force of circumstances'. One must be careful, therefore, not to attribute to the fact that having an obligation differs from being obliged characteristics which are really due to the fact that, for example, having a legal or moral obligation or being legally or morally obliged differs from being obliged by force of circumstances. Thus, Hart's[2] supposition that the statement that a person had an obligation to report for military service may be true irrespective of his beliefs and fears of discovery and punishment, whereas, allegedly, the statement that a man was obliged to hand over his money to a gunman means that he did the latter because of his beliefs and fears does not prove a difference between 'obligation' and 'obliged', but only between 'obligation' and 'obliged by force of circumstances'. For a man may truly be said to be obliged (i.e. legally obliged) to report for military service independently of his beliefs and fears, since what he has a legal obligation to do he is legally obliged to do. Similarly, Hart's assertion that 'whereas the statement that he had this obligation is quite independent of the question whether or not he in fact reported for service, the statement that

[1] e.g. Hart (1961), ch. 5, s. 2; MacCormick (1981), ch. 5, analyses obligation as a requirement due to a personal relationship; Baier (1966), 220a, n. 24, asserts that 'being obliged cannot be used to explain having an obligation'; but his assertion lacks argument.

[2] Loc. cit. In (1982), 145–61, Hart wrongly supposes that to hold that legal and moral rights, duties, and obligations are not necessarily different is to hold that the expressions 'right', 'duty', and 'obligation' have different meanings in legal and moral contexts.

someone was obliged to do something normally carries the implication that he did it' depends for its truth on the type of factor by which one is obliged. One must have done what one was physically obliged to do, but not necessarily what one was legally or morally obliged to to. Prosecuting counsel might well say in 1965 of a doctor who was under contract from 1960 to 1962 that he was obliged by his contract to visit the deceased when telephoned, but that he failed to do so.

Equally mistaken is the common view that a difference in the implications of 'legally or morally obliged' and of 'obliged by force of circumstances' shows a difference in the meaning of 'obliged'.

For instance, one of Hart's arguments is essentially this: 'He was morally (or legally) obliged to V' implies 'He was under an obligation to V', whereas 'He was obliged by the gunman to V' does not imply 'He was under an obligation to V'; therefore, there are two senses of 'oblige'.[3] But this argument is no better than the similarly fallacious argument that because a man who is compelled by orders to retreat retreats 'under compulsion', whereas a man who is compelled by the heat of the flames to retreat does not retreat 'under compulsion', therefore there are two senses of 'compel'; or that because 'The Simonstown Agreement requires us to V' implies 'There is a requirement under the Simonstown Agreement that we V', whereas 'Circumstances requires us to V' does not imply 'There is a requirement that we V', therefore there are two senses of 'require'. A soldier who is ordered to shoot any looters on sight is under orders (has orders) to shoot looters on sight. A soldier on the parade ground who is ordered to pick up his rifle is not under orders (nor has orders) to pick up his rifle. But 'is ordered' is being used in the same sense throughout. Nor is the argument any better than the differently fallacious argument that

[3] Kearney (1972), 47, suggests that Hart meant only to distinguish 'oblige' and 'obligation' and not two senses of 'oblige'. Page (1972) and (1973) certainly uses this argument for two senses of 'oblige'.

because 'The butler was suspected' implies 'The butler was under suspicion', whereas 'Foul play was suspected' does not imply 'Foul play was under suspicion', therefore there are two senses of 'suspect'. The difference in implication between 'He was morally (or legally) obliged' and 'He was obliged by circumstances' can be explained by the kind of factor by which he was obliged. And similarly for 'compel' and 'require'. The difference in implication between 'The butler was suspected' and 'Foul play was suspected' can be explained by the logical difference between that on which the suspicion fell, namely the butler, and that of whose occurrence there was a suspicion, namely foul play. The syntactic differences in the sentences here can be brought out by 'The butler was suspected of foul play' and 'Foul play by the butler was suspected'.

A second argument commonly used to suggest that there are two senses of 'oblige' uses the premisses 'He was obliged by the gunman to V' implies 'He did V', but 'He was obliged by his contract to V' does not imply 'He did V'.[4] The objection to this argument is that by parity of reasoning one would have to invoke two senses of, for example, 'have to', 'require', 'demand'. For it could be argued, first, that 'Owing to the storm everyone *had* to abandon ship' implies that the ship was abandoned, but 'According to the regulations everyone *had* to have two sponsors' does not imply that everyone did have them; secondly, 'Shortage of oxygen *required* us to halt' implies that we did halt, but 'Our contract *required* us to deliver the goods within a fortnight' does not imply that the goods were delivered; thirdly, 'Circumstances *demanded* that he V' implies that he Ved, but 'Honour *demanded* that he V' does not imply that he Ved. Such an extension of ambiguity is fantastic. The solution lies not in two senses of 'oblige', 'have', 'require', or 'demand', but in the different ways in which different factors make things necessary. This is why an out-of-context use of the words 'He was obliged to do it' can leave one in doubt whether what they say

---

[4] e.g. Page (1972) and (1973).

implies that he did it and whether it implies that he was under an obligation to do it.

The ubiquity of the move from a difference in implication to a difference in meaning can easily be shown in philosophical theories about other concepts, such as *responsibility, see,* and *believe.*[5] But, although a word does sometimes have two senses and although this is sometimes the explanation for differences in implication, too easy a recourse to this ploy deflects one's attention from the real source of the difference and, hence, provides only a temporary satisfaction.

(c) *'Obliged by'*

Having argued that common to all the uses of 'oblige' is the idea of being obliged by something, and also that having (or being under) an obligation normally implies being obliged, I want now to examine this notion of being obliged by.

When I am obliged by something, I am obliged by it either to someone or to do something. Both the kindness of the man who opens the door for me and the inconsiderateness of the man who locks it against me (or the faulty mechanism which makes it stick) oblige me. The latter obliges me to do something which can be specified as being any alternative other than the one barred to me by the locked door, while the former obliges me only to him who helped me. I am 'tied' to him, perhaps in goodwill, somewhat as I am 'in his debt' or 'indebted to him', though not obliged to do anything in particular or to pay anything specific.

Though the only thing that can make me obliged to someone is a deed of his, there are many factors which can oblige me to do something specific. I can be obliged by persons, such as a gunman; by circumstances, such as a locked door, ill health, or the inefficiency of a servant; by my own deed, for example the giving of a promise or the assertion of a thesis; by my position, whether as a secretary or a doctor; or by rules and regulations, for example of morals, the law, or

[5] Cp. White (1971).

a club. Sometimes the obliging factor is not mentioned, but only what I am obliged to do; for example to give my full name and address, to offer either examination paper X or paper Y, if I offer paper D.

Ordinarily a person of a certain position, in certain circumstances, with certain aims and following certain rules of conduct, has some freedom of choice. There are various alternative ways in which he can behave compatibly with his position, circumstances, aims, and rules. Within this sphere he can do whatever he wants. A yachtsman intent on making port may have several alternative routes; there may be no agreed date on which a manufacturer has to deliver his goods, a candidate's choice of papers may be fairly unrestricted, a chess player may have several possible moves. In different circumstances, however, a factor may be present or may intervene which limits this choice by leaving him with no alternative, compatible with his general position, but to do so and so. He is now obliged by this factor to do so and so. This factor ties or binds him to doing it; it makes it necessary for him to do it. The wind obliges the yachtsman to alter course; the terms of his contract oblige the manufacturer to deliver his goods within a fortnight; the degree regulations oblige the student who offers paper D to choose either paper X or paper Y; a particular move by his opponent may oblige a chess player to move his king. As the case of the student shows, what one is obliged to do may be to choose within a restricted field rather than to take without choice. Similarly, the man who is under an obligation because of a promise given or who has obligations to his children or his allies is restricted, in a specified or unspecified way, in regard to his future acts. I may not be free to dine with you because I have promised to visit someone else; my country may have no choice but to go to war, if its allies are attacked.

What I am obliged to do is not something I cannot help doing or something I am unable not to do. I may sometimes quite easily not do what I am obliged to do. It is something I am unable not to do without incurring certain consequences.

There is always an 'otherwise' in the offing.[6] I have to do what I am obliged to do, otherwise these consequences will follow. The manufacturer who is legally obliged by his contract to deliver the goods within a fortnight can only not do so at the cost of breaking the law. The man who promises to do X can only not do X by infringing some moral rule. Where one is obliged by force of circumstances, the 'otherwise' in the offing is the loss of some specific objective. The yachtsman who is obliged to alter course can only not do so by throwing away his chance of reaching port; the traveller who is obliged to hand over his wallet to the gunman can only avoid doing so by giving up his life. It is always possible to act incompatibly with the legal or moral situation or with one's objectives. But given that there is no alteration in these, one is in the stated circumstances obliged to follow a certain course. The question whether someone has a choice or not does not occur in a vacuum, but in a particular situation. The question is whether, in this situation, I am obliged to do X or whether, physically, legally, or morally, I may choose X or an alternative. It is a different question whether I have a choice between doing X and either giving up my objective or behaving illegally or immorally. What I am physically obliged to do is what, given adherence to physical conditions and to my objective, I have physically no option but to do. What I have a moral or legal obligation to do is what, given my situation and the moral or legal conditions, I have no moral or legal option but to do. The obliging factor narrows down what I can physically, legally, or morally do. There is, of course, no suggestion that what legally or morally one is obliged or has to do is what physically one is obliged or has to do or that a narrowing of one's legal or moral options is a narrowing of one's physical options. What I am legally or morally obliged to do can conflict either with something else I am also legally or morally obliged to do or with something I am physically obliged to do, though I cannot be physically obliged to do conflicting things, since what I am physically

[6] Cp. Nowell-Smith (1954), 202.

obliged to do, unlike what I am legally or morally obliged to do, I in fact do.

To be obliged to do something is not to have something done to one. The yachtsman is obliged to alter course, he is not swept off it. The gunman obliges me to hand over my wallet, he does not snatch it from me. To be obliged to do something is quite unlike being physically compelled to do something, even when the obliging factor is a physical event such as a fall of snow on the railway line by which I had hoped to travel. For a physical compulsion, unlike an obliging factor, turns a deed done by me into something done to me. When I am obliged, I still have a choice and am still called upon to act, but the choice is not among alternatives at the same level as the obligatory alternative. At that level, I must take the obligatory one. The difference between what I do because I am obliged to do it and what I do because I choose to do it is not the difference between a choice and a free choice,[7] but between a choice whether or not to act inconsistently with one's general position and a choice among alternatives compatible with one's general position. If I am obliged to alter course, I do not choose this course from alternatives, though neither is it impossible for me not to take it. I alter course because, given that I do not want to be driven out to sea, I have physically no choice but to. I am tied to this course. The fact that I could choose to let myself be driven out to sea is irrelevant, since the original problem was whether, given that I did not want to be driven out to sea, I had any choice of course. Similarly, the manufacturer is obliged to deliver the goods within a fortnight because, given that he is to fulfil his contract, he has legally no choice but to deliver by that date.

Hence, there is no paradox in saying that a man who is obliged to do X has no choice, even though it is physically possible for him—and perhaps quite easy—not to do X.[8]

What I do thinking I am obliged to do it, I do; it is not

[7] e.g. Nowell-Smith (1954), 202; cp. Gauthier, 176.
[8] Cp. Nowell-Smith (1954), 201; Hart and Honoré, 72.

something done to me. Yet I do not do it voluntarily. To say[9] that I was obliged voluntarily to do so and so is a contradiction. I do not do it voluntarily because I do not choose to do it in preference to another alternative; I was, I thought, tied to it by the obliging factor. What I voluntarily do is contrasted with what I do thinking I am obliged to do it and not, except by philosophers and jurisprudents, with what is done to me.[10] A trade-union member may give a voluntary subscription to charity, but he is obliged to subscribe to his union fund; a man may give himself up voluntarily or because he thinks he is obliged to do so; a student may withdraw voluntarily from the university or be obliged to withdraw. Contrast answering because you were asked a direct question and volunteering the information. The contrast between a voluntary and an obligatory subscription, surrender, or withdrawal is not the same as the contrast between a voluntary payment and a levy, a voluntary surrender and a capture, or a voluntary withdrawal and expulsion. For the former is a contrast between one thing I do and another that I do, one voluntarily and the other obligatorily, while the latter is a contrast between what I do and what is done to me. What I do thinking I am obliged to do it, I do not voluntarily do; since I think I have to do it. What is done to me I do not voluntarily do, since I do not do it at all.

It is these two contrasts which, it seems to me, Aristotle distinguishes in the opening sections of the third book of the *Nicomachean Ethics*; i.e. (i) the contrast between throwing one's goods overboard to save oneself in a storm and throwing them overboard voluntarily, and (ii) the contrast between being carried out to sea by the wind and putting out to sea.

Further, if what I do is unintentional, unknowing, or in some respects non-attentive, it is neither voluntary nor obliged, though it is still a deed of mine. If, by a voluntary remark of mine, I quite unintentionally hurt your feelings,

[9] e.g. Gauthier, 176.
[10] e.g. Aristotle, *NE* III. i; Nowell-Smith (1954), 201; Gauthier, 176; Ryle, 73-4.

I did not hurt them voluntarily nor was I obliged to hurt them. If, by voluntarily handing over a letter to you, I give you a secret document by mistake, I did not voluntarily or non-voluntarily pass on secret information. What I do absent-mindedly is neither voluntary nor obliged.

The contrast between an act and a happening is one way in which *being obliged* is different from *being bound*. I can only be obliged to do something, whereas I can be bound either to do or to feel something or to have something happen to me. I can be bound, but not obliged, to succeed or to fail, to cry or to feel tired. I can be obliged to surrender, but only bound to be caught; obliged to jump, but only bound to fall. Since inanimate objects do not perform actions, they can only be bound to do what they do. The shopkeeper may be obliged to raise his prices, but his prices can only be bound to go up. If I am obliged to do so and so, I have no alternative to doing it other than acting incompatibly with my moral, legal, or desired position. If something is bound to happen, there is no alternative to its happening unless some other part of the situation is altered. Thus, the inhabitants are bound to be massacred unless the relief column arrives before nightfall; it is bound to rain unless the wind changes. Whereas 'obliged' carries an 'otherwise' rider, 'bound' has an 'unless' rider.

Many philosophers have suggested that the alternative which I am obliged to take must be less desirable, less desired, or less advantageous than the other alternatives;[11] that 'the logic of obligation requires a conflict between the obligation to do something and the inclination not to do it'.[12] This is a mistake. Being in the position of being able to choose among alternatives, of being able to do whatever I want, is more desirable and perhaps more desired than being restricted in my choice by having to do something whether I want to or not. But it does not follow from this that the alternative

[11] e.g. Nowell-Smith (1954), 206 ff.; Hart (1961), 80, 85; Gauthier, 177-9; Baier (1966), 212a.
[12] Nowell-Smith (1954), 210-11; cp. Kant.

to which I am restricted is less desirable or desired than the alternatives once open to me; nor that I cannot be said to be obliged to do what is advantageous to me. A candidate who wishes to offer paper D may be obliged to choose his further option from papers X and Y, but this need not be a less desirable course to him than choosing between papers P and Q. To be free to live either within or without the city boundary is more desirable than to be obliged to live within it; but there need be no suggestion that it is less desirable to live where one is obliged to live than to live elsewhere. The fact that exchanging a pawn for a queen or other piece is an advantage in chess does not preclude this change's being obligatory in certain circumstances.[13] It is simply false to suppose that 'to say to someone that he had an obligation to refrain from torturing children plainly implies that he would want to torture them if he had a chance'.[14] Often, of course, the obligatory action is less pleasing than the alternatives and is one which I would not have taken if I could have avoided it; but not necessarily so. Furthermore, even when the obligatory course is undesirable, it is not this quality which makes it obligatory, but the fact that it is the course I am tied to in the circumstances. It is not the fact that I consider a visit to the dentist undesirable *per se* that allows me to say I am obliged to go,[15] but the fact that it is the only course open to a person who wants to stop his toothache or, perhaps, who has promised to go. The obligatory course is the course I have to take whether I want to or not; not the course I would not take unless I had to. It is not a question of whether I want the course or not; since the course is obligatory, that question does not arise. The fact that we often excuse ourselves by pleading that what we did was not what we wanted to do but only what we were obliged to do does not show that being obliged to do something implies not wanting to do it.[16] Nor is it relevant whether the end to which the obliged alternative may be a means is pleasant or

---

[13] *Pace* Gauthier, 177.
[15] e.g. Gauthier, 178.
[14] Baier (1966), 212a.
[16] *Pace* Nowell-Smith (1954), 206.

unpleasant.[17] If I have only five minutes to get through my dinner before an appointment, I shall be obliged to rush through the meal irrespective of whether the appointment is for an evening at the theatre or for a boring committee meeting. Nor is it necessary for me to have an interest in, or concern about, keeping the appointment.[18] It is keeping the appointment that contributes to the obligatoriness of my haste.

Nor should we confuse, as some philosophers have done, the circumstances which may oblige me to do something and a general objective whose preservation may depend on my doing the obliged action.[19] In virtue of my general objective I may have several alternatives open; I am not obliged to take any particular one of them. What obliges me to take one of them is that factor which closes the others and ties me to this one. It is the wind, and not his desire to avoid being swept out to sea, which obliges the yachtsman to alter course. Certainly, I would not do the obligatory deed unless I wished to attain my objective, and sometimes it is necessary to mention what this objective is. Thus, I may be obliged to support a colleague on one measure on Senate because I want his support on another. But to say that I am obliged to do X if, or because, I want Y, or in order to get Y, is not to say that it is the desire for Y which obliges me to do X, or that I am obliged to do X by my desire for Y. My desire for Y is not the obliging factor. What does oblige me to do X is that factor which rules out any alternative ways of getting the desired Y. What obliges me to support my colleague on Senate is not the desire to have his support in return, but the fact or the knowledge that his support of me is dependent on my support of him. This fact or knowledge limits my choice of means of getting his support. I know that only by supporting him can I get him to support me. What obliges me to do X partly explains why I do X, but it is a mistake to suppose

[17] e.g. Gauthier, 178.
[18] e.g. Page (1972) and (1973).
[19] e.g. Gauthier, 179 ff.; cp. Austin (1861), xxii–xxiii.

that it is my reason or motive for doing X;[20] or that being obliged to do X means doing X in order to get or preserve Y. I already have my general reason or motive for doing X, namely a desire for Y, which is a reason for doing whatever is a means to Y. What the obliging factor does is to restrict my choice of means by tying me to certain ones. Motives or reasons do not oblige me to do anything. Hence, there is no need to try to distinguish obliging from non-obliging motives (e.g. Nowell-Smith) or the kinds of reasons for action that motives provide from the kinds of reasons that obligations provide (e.g. Gauthier).

Because the law actually attaches sanctions and penalties to failure to do what one is legally obliged to do, jurisprudents and moral philosophers have sometimes identified the obliging factors in law with the sanctions, and supposed that to say that one is legally obliged to do so and so means that it has to be done in order to avoid unpleasant consequences.[21] But this is a mistake. Sanctions are not legal bonds; they are measures employed to strengthen these bonds. To be physically obliged, for example by a fall of snow, to take one rail route rather than any other is to have the alternatives physically closed, thus making it a physical impossibility to take any alternative other than the obligatory one, though not, of course, physically impossible to abstain from action altogether. To be legally obliged, on the other hand, for example by railway regulations, to take one route rather than any other is to have the alternatives only legally closed. There need be no physical difficulty in taking an alternative other than the legally obligatory one. Hence, the law usually introduces sanctions and penalties to prevent people from doing, or to punish them for doing, what it is legally, though not physically, obligatory not to do. But reference to such a sanction is no part of the meaning of 'legally obligatory'. Similarly, any reference to the part played by social pressures or qualms of conscience in getting

[20] e.g. Gauthier, 183; Nowell-Smith (1954), 204; Hart (1961), 80.
[21] e.g. Austin (1851), xxii–xxiii; Nowell-Smith (1954), 200, 204, 209, 242.

people to do what is morally obligatory is quite irrelevant to the meaning of 'morally obligatory'.[22]

(d) Obliged *and* ought

'Obligation' and 'obliged', like 'duty', can no more be equated with, or explained by, 'ought', as many philosophers[23] and jurisprudents[24] attempt to do, than can 'must' be equated with, or explained by, 'ought'. 'Obliged' ('obligation'), like 'must', indicates, as we saw, that because of a particular requirement, whether legal, economic, prudential, or moral, the features of the situation are such that the agent has only one course open to him; the obligatory course is necessary because it is the course he is tied to. 'Ought', by contrast, indicates that in the situation one of several courses open is the right or the best course.[25] Given certain circumstances and a requirement, no question of what he ought to do arises for the yachtsman who is physically obliged by the wind to change course or for the manufacturer who is legally obliged by his contract to deliver the goods by a specified date. Advice can be given to someone in the form of a statement about what he ought to do because such a statement differentiates between the merits of alternatives; but to tell someone what in the circumstances he is obliged to do is only to give him information about which course is the only one open to him.

Where one has conflicting ends which would oblige one to take contradictory courses, one can ask oneself from a different point of view, which end, if any, one either ought

---

[22] *Pace* Hart (1961), 84–5.

[23] e.g. Prichard (1949), 89–91; Hare (1963), 170; von Wright (1963); Baier (1958); Black (1964); Grice; Zink, ch. 4. Ewing (1947) equates 'obligation' with what he calls one sense of 'ought'; contrast Nowell-Smith (1954), ch. 14 and Gauthier, ch. 12. Ross (1939), chs. 3–4, distinguishes 'right' and 'obligatory', but seems to equate 'obligatory' both with 'the right thing' and with 'ought', cp. (1930), 3. Sesonske's criticism of the obligation/evaluation assimilation expressly denies any correlation of this difference with specific linguistic differences.

[24] e.g. Smith (1976).

[25] Many philosophers slip from 'best' to 'only' or 'necessary' in their analyses of *ought*; e.g. von Wright, Black, Gauthier, Diggs.

to or is obliged to pursue. Thus, I may know that if I try to climb a hill, its steepness will oblige me to change gear and also know that if I am to save my gearbox, its faulty condition will oblige me to stay in the same gear. I have, therefore, to ask myself whether I ought, or am obliged, to try to climb the hill and thus damage the gearbox or to try to save the gearbox and thus fail to climb the hill. Where one has conflicting legal or moral obligations, one is legally or morally obliged to do both of the things one has an obligation to do. Hence, from a different point of view, the only question can be which of the two one ought to do. Thus, my promise to my wife may oblige me to be home for dinner, while my duty as a doctor may oblige me to stay late at the hospital. Ought I to leave the hospital early to keep my promise and so fail in my duty as a doctor or stay at the hospital to do my duty as a doctor and so break my promise to my wife? Only from some other point of view can I find out what I ought to do.

Any attempt to discover a necessary connection between a statement about what one ought to do and a statement about what one is obliged (or under an obligation) to do is doomed to failure.[26] It involves *either* the sensible, but admittedly too weak, supposition that because according to one requirement, for example of a promise made or a desire for economy, one is obliged to do so and so, therefore, when all things are taken into consideration one ought to do it; *or* the nonsensical, because too strong, supposition that because according to one requirement, for example of a promise made or a desire for economy, one is obliged to do so and so, therefore, by the same requirement, one ought to do it. Although the same thing can be for one reason something I ought to do, and for another something I am obliged to do, as when I am obliged because of my office to do what I ought as a matter of courtesy to do anyway, *ought* and *obliged* are in relation to one and the same reason, mutually exclusive—though not exhaustive—since the

[26] e.g. Searle (1969), 180-1.

former implies that there are, and the latter implies that there are not, alternative courses of action. This is why we can set at rest anyone's worry whether he has done the right or the best thing by assuring him that he has done the only thing.

The notion that morally speaking one *ought* to do so and so differs from the notion that morally speaking one *must* or *is obliged* to do it in the same way as that in which these notions differ in non-moral contexts. Depending on the features of the situation and on our moral code, there will be some things one ought to do and others one is obliged to do.[27] Status, position, office, duties, and commitments normally carry with them certain obligations, while the features of alternative courses and actions normally show one of them to be the appropriate one, the one we ought to choose. To hold that one ought, rather than that one is obliged, to keep one's promises sounds too weak; whereas to hold that one is obliged, rather than that one ought, to go to the help of the traveller set upon by thieves sounds too strong. At the very least, it suggests a different conception of the moral life. It is because some philosophers have subscribed to the very general principle that morally the thing one must do is that which, all other things being considered, is the right or the best thing to do that they have made what one is obliged to do and what one ought to do necessarily coincident.[28] But to say that the morally owing (or the right or the best) course—what we ought to do— is the morally tying (or necessary) course—what we are obliged to do—is not to utter a tautology. The idea of being *owing*—morally or otherwise—that is, the idea expressed by 'ought', and the idea of being *tying*—morally or otherwise—that is, the idea expressed by 'obliged', are distinct ideas.

[27] Cp. Hart (1958) and Sesonske.
[28] e.g. Moore (1903), s. 89, 'the assertion "I am morally bound to perform" is identical with the assertion "This action will produce the greatest amount of good in the universe" '.

(e) Obligation *and* duty

Finally, let us look at the similarities and differences between the two notions of *duty* and *obligation*, which we have seen are frequently assimilated to each other by philosophers and jurisprudents.

An important way in which the notion of *duty* is like those of *obligation* and *being obliged*, but unlike that of *ought*, is that what one has a duty to do, like what one has an obligation or is obliged to do, but unlike what one ought to do, depends not on the nature or consequences of what is to be done, but on the antecedent circumstances of the agent. It is because cruelty to children is evil in itself or produces bad results that I ought not to be cruel to children; but my duty or obligation to be kind to the children entrusted to my care or whom I have promised to look after arises from this position of trust or this promise. The close connection of both *duty* and *obligation* with the agent in contrast to the connection of *ought* with the deed accounts for the fact that though what one has a right to do may, in certain circumstances, be something one ought not to do, it cannot be something one has a duty or obligation not to do. Duties share with obligations and with factors which oblige the characteristic that they can be of a moral, a social, a legal, or an institutional kind. I can have moral, legal, and family duties and obligations as I can be morally, legally, or by family relationships obliged. Duties, like obligations or what I am obliged to do, can be imposed on me or assumed by me. Neither duties nor obligations—or what I am obliged to do —are, despite what is commonly asserted, necessarily related to sanctions, however usual and useful the latter are to punish those who fail to do what they have a duty, an obligation, or are obliged to do. Duties are also like obligations in their contrast to rights, especially in their possible subjects and objects. Only human beings, and perhaps only sufficiently adult human beings or collections of them like the state or a county council, can have—or are even usually argued to have—duties or obligations, whereas it is, as we shall see, at least arguable—and certainly often argued—that the possession of rights can be extended to children, babies, foetuses, animals, and even inanimate nature. Equally, one can have a duty or an obligation, but not usually a right, to a person; and a right, but not usually a duty or an obligation, to a thing.

There are, I think, only two main ways in which duties are like obligations, but unlike what one is obliged to do. First, though one can have a moral or legal duty or obligation or be morally or legally obliged, one cannot have a physical or logical duty any more than a physical or logical obligation as one can be obliged by force of physical or logical circumstances. The snowfall on the railway line may oblige one to travel by bus just as assuming one set of premises may oblige one to accept a particular conclusion, but neither imposes on one an obligation or duty to do what one is obliged to do. Secondly, and relatedly, duties, like obligations but unlike much—though not all—of what one may be obliged to do, are often imposed by rules, whether statutory or customary.

The differences between *duty*, on the one hand, and either *obligation* or *being obliged*, on the other, are, however, more numerous than their similarities. The notion of something due, which is central to duty, is different from the notion of something bound, which is central to obligation.[29] What I have a duty to do is what is laid on me, perhaps because of my job, to do; what I have an obligation to do is what I am tied to and have no alternative to doing. One's obligations are something one meets, as one meets requirements; one's duties are something one performs, as one performs tasks. Duties, but not obligations, can be allocated; obligations, but not duties, can be incurred. One's duty can comprise, as Bradley suggests, a set of duties; but one's obligation does

---

[29] Feinberg's (1970) excursus (p. 244) into the etymology of 'duty' seems to misinterpret this relation. Whiteley (1953) derives both duty and obligation from a trust-relationship.

not comprise a set of obligations. Hence, so and so can be part of one's duty, but not part of one's obligation.

One can have an obligation without a duty. Thus, my promising to do something for you or your having done a favour for me may lay me under an obligation, but not necessarily make anything my duty. Nor is my obligation under the railway statutes not to break my journey a duty. On the other hand, if one has a duty, for example to distribute the mail, though it may be that one is, therefore, obliged—and has or is under an obligation—to do it, nevertheless, though delivering the mail is one's duty, it is not one's obligation. To say that my main duty as a half-back is to stop the opposing centre forward or as a time-keeper to record the arrival of the workers is not to say that these are my obligations, even though it may be because these are my duties that I am obliged to do them. Since a common way in which obligations arise is because of contracts in which parties bind themselves, while duties are often laid on one by the state or some other giver of office, the notion of obligation is more common in contract law and that of duty more common in criminal law and the tort of negligence.

These differences between *duty* and *obligation*—and also the temptation to assimilate them—are to be explained by the fact that 'obligation' signifies the relation of a necessity, requirement, or bond one has to do so and so, whereas 'duty' signifies one reason, namely that it is something due, perhaps because of one's position or job, which may make the performance of this deed a necessity. Thus one's duty may oblige one to do so and so. One may, as we say, be 'in duty bound' to do it as one can be 'in honour bound' to do it. But an obligation cannot make the doing of so and so one's duty. One can sensibly talk of being obliged by duty, but not having a duty because of an obligation. What the common assimilation of *duty* and *obligation* has done is to confuse the relation of binding, which can be caused by various factors, including one's duty, with one factor, namely duty, which can bind or oblige one.

5

Rights, Duties, and Obligations

Philosophers and jurisprudents have commonly suggested various connections between rights and duties. Sometimes they have sought the grounds of one in the existence of the other;[1] sometimes they have attempted a definition of one by the other;[2] and sometimes they have suggested that a right in one person and a duty in another are correlatives or even two sides of the same coin.[3] The language in which these alleged relationships between rights and duties is expressed is in fact very various, especially among jurisprudents. It includes such phrases as 'resulting out of', 'springs', and 'exists from' (Bentham); 'rests on' and 'whenever . . .' (Austin); 'based on', 'derived from', and 'give rise to' (Salmond); 'historical origin' (Vinogradoff); 'conditions' (Hart); 'based on', 'at the root of', 'generate', 'determine', 'substrate', and 'test' (Dias); 'depends on' (MacCormick). Because frequently, as we have seen, no distinction is made by philosophers and jurisprudents between a duty and an obligation, analogous theses are also advocated about the relations between rights and obligations.[4] There may be a slight tendency for philosophers to concentrate on the relations between rights and obligations and jurisprudents on those between rights and duties. But the arguments are substantially the same and are open to the same objections. For this reason I shall usually consider them together.

Rights and duties (or obligations) differ both in what can

[1] e.g. Austin (1861), I. 398; Salmond (1924), 240; Allen (1931), 183–93; Cranston (1973), 68; Keeton (1949); Kelsen (1941).

[2] Bentham (Bowring ed., III. 181, 217-18); Raphael (1967), 54–67; Dworkin (1977a), 159.

[3] e.g. Lamont (1946), ch. 3; Benn and Peters (1959), ch. 4; Radin (1938); Bradley (1876), ch. v; Jenks (1933), ch. 8; Kocourek (1927), ch. I; Paton (1974), ch. 12; Pollock (1929), 61–70.

[4] e.g. Brandt (1959), 438; Postow (1977).

be the objects of one or the other and what can be the subjects of one or the other.

What we have duties (or obligations) to and what we have rights to are different. We can have duties (or obligations), but not usually rights, to persons; and rights, but not usually duties—much less obligations—to things. For having a duty (or obligation) to somebody implies having a duty (or obligation) to do something for him, whereas having a right to something—or even to somebody—implies having a right to its possession. Having a duty to something such as one's science or one's art or, perhaps, one's country—to none of which, perhaps, we have an obligation—is an exception that proves the rule, for these are not things to which one can have a right. Furthermore, though whenever we can have a duty (or obligation) to V—where 'V' is a verb—it at least makes sense to say we can have a right to V, it is not true that whenever we can have a right to V, it makes sense to say that we can have a duty (or obligation) to V. We can, for example, have a right, but not a duty (or obligation), to receive something, such as to be protected or fed, or to feel something, such as depressed or angry, or to have an attitude, such as to think, assume, or expect so and so. Our duties (or obligations), but not our rights, are, as we saw, confined to what we can be said to be capable of *doing*.

Equally what can have a right and what can have a duty (or obligation) are in some cases definitely, and in some cases arguably, different. Adult human beings can have both rights and duties (or obligations). But whereas it is, as we shall see, arguable—and certainly has often been argued—that rights may be possessed by other than adult human beings, whether they be generations yet unborn, children, babies, human foetuses, animals, or even objects in nature, it is never suggested that natural objects, animals, foetuses, babies, or unborn generations have duties (or obligations).

The question whether rights and duties (or obligations) are in any way logically related can arise either when it is one and the same person's rights and duties (or obligations) we are examining or when it is the right of one person and the duty (or obligation) of another.

(a) One person's rights and duties (or obligations)

It is possible for someone who has a right to V also to have a duty (or obligation) to V, as when someone who sees a wrong being done may have both the right and the duty to speak up or when a judge has both a right and a duty to direct the jury on certain points. People often insist that a certain course of action is not only their right—and, therefore, something which they can but need not do—but also their duty—and, therefore, something they needs must do. The courts have held that an operation to save a mother's life may be both the right and the duty of a gynaecologist[5] and that the disclosure of a felony is both a citizen's right and duty.[6]

On the other hand, one's right to V does not necessarily, as is sometimes suggested,[7] impose on its possessor any duty (or obligation) to V; nor does one's duty (or obligation) to V necessarily impose any right to V. Some things one can have a right to, for example to enter a public place or to erect a fence around one's garden, without necessarily having a duty to. It is a purely contingent matter that some states, such as ancient Athens or modern El Salvador, impose a duty to vote on all who have a right to. Other things one can, as we saw, have a right to, for example to have something given to one, to feel something or to have a certain attitude, without its even making sense to say that we have a duty (or obligation) to them. It is also at least arguable, as we hinted, that there are creatures, such as infants, idiots, and animals, who can have rights, though they cannot have duties.[8]

---

[5] *R* v. *Bourne* [1939] 1 KB 687 *per* MacNaughton, J.
[6] *Thorne* v. *Motor Trade Association* [1937] AC 797 *per* Atkin, LJ.
[7] e.g. Bradley (1876), ch. v. note; Benn and Peters (1959), 90.
[8] e.g. Feinberg (1978); contrast Ritchie (1894), 109 ff., who argues against animals' rights on the ground that they cannot have duties.

Equally, though one's duty (or obligation) to do something may give one grounds for a right to do it or something connected with it, as when the duty of parishioners to attend church sustained their claim to a right to enter it,[9] one can, nevertheless, have a duty without a right. An obvious case is where one has a duty (or obligation) to someone, though no question arises of having a right to him. Further, though frequently whenever one has a duty (or obligation) to do something, for example to examine the firm's accounts or to send one's children to school, one also has a right to do it —and this may be why we sometimes meet the denial that we have a right to V by insisting that, indeed, we have a positive duty to V—this is not always so. The authority who imposes on a spy the duty to photograph the enemy's papers cannot give him the right to do so; a right which he certainly does not have from any other source. A citizen may have a duty to vote at a time when he lacks the right because he has not filled in the electoral roll which alone gives him this right. Making a promise to someone places me under an obligation—and, perhaps, imposes on me a duty—both to him and to do what I have promised; but not only does it clearly not give me a right to him, it also does not give me a right to do what I have promised to do.

Bentham and some modern writers have attempted to relate one and the same person's rights and duties (or obligations) in rather a different way. They have suggested that a ground, a necessary and sufficient condition, or even the meaning, of someone's having a right to V is the same person's having *no* duty (or obligation) *not* to V.[10] But this confuses the notions of *right* and *liberty*.[11] The absence of a duty (or obligation) not to V is not a sufficient condition of the right to V, since there are many things which I have no duty (or obligation) not to do, for example to criticize my betters, to

---

[9] *Cole* v. *Police Constable 443A* [1937] 1 KB 316 at 330.

[10] e.g. Bowring III, 181, 217-18; (1789), ch. xvi. 26; cp. Raphael (1967), 54-67; Dworkin (1977a), 189; Wringe (1981), 46.

[11] Hart (1973), 174 ff., compromises by allowing these as 'liberty rights'; cp. (1955), 179.

ask favours of strangers, to enter a foreign country and am, therefore, free to do, but which I nevertheless do not have a right to do. Contrapositively, not having a right to V does not, as this theory would have to allow, entail having a duty (or obligation) not to V. There are many things I lack a right to do, for example to take my place at the head of the queue, to sue for recovery of so and so, which nevertheless I do not have a duty (or obligation) to refrain from doing. Hence, there is no such right as Bentham's 'right resulting from the absence of obligation'. Nor is the absence of a contrary duty (or obligation) a necessary condition of having a right, since there are many things, for example to know so and so, to feel such and such, to be given or provided with this or that, which I have a right to, but which even holders of this thesis admit it makes no sense to say that I have no duty (or obligation) not to do. Only where I can properly be said to have no duty (or obligation) not to V does this follow from my having a right to V, and, hence, only in this area is the absence of a duty (or obligation) not to V a necessary condition, though still not a sufficient condition, of a right to V.

It may be that this false thesis—namely that the absence of a duty (or obligation) not to V implies the presence of a right to V—partly results from confusion with the legitimate thesis that the presence of a duty (or obligation) not to V implies the absence of a right to V. This is, of course, simply to make the mistake of concluding from 'If p, then q' to 'If not p, then not q'.

(b) The rights of one and the duties (or obligations) of another

Philosophers and jurisprudents have usually been more interested not in the relations between the rights and duties (or obligations) of one person, but in the relations between the rights of one and the duties (or obligations) of another, and conversely. Many have held that one person's right is correlative with, is the necessary or sufficient ground of, or is the other side of the same coin as, another person's duty (or obligation).[12]

It can, of course, happen that when I have a right to receive something, there may be someone on whom a duty (or obligation) is laid to provide it, and, equally, that when I have a duty (or obligation) to provide something, the recipient has a right to receive it. This frequently happens when I have a right to receive payment for a debt and you have a duty (or obligation) to repay it or when I have a duty (or obligation) to give what I promised and you have a right to be given it. The rights and duties of husband and wife or of employer and employee are often reciprocal in this way. But there need be no logically necessary connections between the several rights and duties themselves, which arise from the total common situation.

Moreover, one person's duty (or obligation) to do something is often not accompanied by any reciprocal right in another person.

One reason for this is that, as we saw in an earlier chapter, there can be a duty to do *something*, for example a judge's duty to pass sentence, a doctor's duty to keep records of his patients, a porter's duty to take down the names of visitors, or a policeman's duty to report offenders, which is not a duty to *someone* and, therefore, gives rise to no right in any one. Moral and religious codes, such as the *Decalogue*, commonly lay down duties without conferring any corresponding rights. Such duties to do something, which are nevertheless not duties to anyone, may even include duties to do something to someone, as when it is my duty to punish an offender, to stop the opposing centre forward, to expose someone's felony[13] or, in a totalitarian country, to inform on my parents. It would be queer to suggest that, because of

---

[12] e.g. Bradley (1876), Essay V; Lamont (1946), ch. 3; Benn and Peters (1959), ch. 4; Salmond (1924), ch. 10; Jenks (1933), ch. 8; Kocourek (1927), ch. I; Paton (1974), ch. 12; MacDonald (1947), 239; Ritchie (1894), 98; Frankena (1955); P. C. Williams (1976).

[13] e.g. *Sykes* v. *D.P.P.* [1961] 3 All ER 33 *per* Denning LJ.

my duty, the offender has a right to be punished, the centre forward a right to be stopped, or the felon or my parents a right to be informed on. To say that it is the duty of the prosecution to produce evidence against the defendant is hardly to suggest that the defendant has a right that the prosecution should produce this. A prisoner of war's duty to escape does not imply his captor's right to help him to escape, nor does the captor's duty to prevent him escaping imply the prisoner's right to be prevented. Even Bentham, who thought some duties involved rights, confined these to what he called 'extra-regarding' duties and Mill distinguished between 'duties of perfect obligation' which he thought involved rights and 'duties of imperfect obligation' which he thought did not.[14]

Also among the duties to do something, which are not duties to anyone, are included duties to do something *for* someone, as when a daughter has a duty to perform household services for her father's guests or an employee for his employer's customers. Whatever the position of the second party, that is the father or the employer, these third parties, that is the guests or the customers, do not necessarily have any rights in virtue of the first party's duties. It is, as we saw earlier, a mistake to suppose that that which we have a duty (or obligation) to do something *for* must be something we have a duty (or obligation) *to*.[15] This mistake is clear not only in this case of the daughter or employee, but more so when what one has a duty to do something for is something which either one certainly or one debatedly could not have a duty to, as when one has a duty to do something for the preservation of Venice or for the protection of foxes. Hence, even if it were plausible to argue from A's duty to B to B's right, this would not show that one could argue from A's duty to do something for B to B's right.

Secondly, even where one person has not only a duty either to do something or to do something for someone, but

---

[14] e.g. Bentham (1945), 36; Mill, *Utilitarianism*, ch. v.
[15] e.g. Rachels (1976), 223.

also a duty *to* someone, the one to whom he has such a duty does not necessarily thereby acquire any corresponding right. A doctor has certain duties to his patients, a teacher to his pupils, and a sovereign to his subjects which do not give them any rights, however 'extra-regarding' these duties may be, as when the doctor dutifully does not indulge the patient's desire for drugs, the teacher keeps his pupil's nose to the grindstone, and the sovereign sees that his subjects are always militarily prepared. Even if we have duties to animals and to infants, it is debatable whether they can have rights.[16]

If we have duties to the dead, for example to tend their graves or not to slander their memory, it does not follow that they have a corresponding right.[17] If I can have a duty to myself—which, of course, some philosophers dispute[18]— such as to look after my health, I do not, as even Bentham, who allowed duties to oneself, admitted, thereby have a right to receive something from myself. Certainly, one can have a duty to one's art or to science without one's art or science having a right.

Nor is it legitimate to try to circumvent these cases of one person's having a duty, either to someone or to do something, where the person, animal, or thing affected has clearly no correlative right, by suggesting that either the person or body imposing the duty or the public at large has the right to the performance of that duty.[19] Any such right which the authority might have could not be a right to be Ved correlative to my duty to V.

As philosophers have supposed about moral rights and duties (or obligations), so jurisprudents have supposed about legal rights and duties (or obligations) that one man's duty implies another man's right.[20] But this is clearly not so in

[16] Cp. Salmond (1957), 263; Ross (1930), 48 ff.; Pound (1959), IV. 182; contrast, e.g., Feinberg (1978).

[17] *Pace* McLachlan (1977), 199.

[18] e.g. Hart (1958), 180.

[19] e.g. Salmond (1951), 292; Holland (1885), 406; Keeton (1949), 134-5; Paton (1946), 217-19. Contrast Pound (1959), IV. 183-5; Allen (1931), 184; Austin (1861), I. 401.

[20] e.g. Austin (1861), I. 398; Salmond (1924), 240; Allen (1931), 183-93.

law. As Mill objected, the fact that the law has a duty to punish a convicted criminal does not give him any right to be punished. Admittedly, when A owes a duty to B to do so and so, it may well be that B has a right to have so and so done. And it is often important in the law, especially on questions of negligence, to discover to whom someone has a certain duty. Has the manufacturer of bottled drinks a duty of care to the ultimate consumers of those drinks?[21] Has the repairer of a lift a duty of care to all those who use it?[22]

But someone can have a legal duty to do so and so without owing this duty to anyone, who might, thus, have gained a right. If A contracts with B to do something for B and C, then A has a duty to do it for B and C. He may even have a duty to B. But he has none to C and C has not thereby been given any right, even though in some kinds of contracts third parties can have rights.[23] The criminal law is full of duties laid on every citizen, for example not to carry offensive weapons in a public place, to insure his car or to observe road signs, which contain no reference to duties to other people and, therefore, in no way imply corresponding rights in others. Even Austin admitted the existence of the so-called 'absolute duties', which include, for example, the duty not to commit suicide, to do military service, to abstain from cruelty to animals.[24] Such a duty, he said, 'neither implies, nor is implied by, a right'. In early United States laws the masters of slaves had absolute duties towards them, as towards animals, but the slaves had no rights.[25] Duties created by statute are often unaccompanied by any corresponding rights. Thus, a breach of duty by the Prison Authorities need not deprive a prisoner of any rights,[26] nor can A be freed from his statutory duty, for example not to

---

[21] *Donoghue* v. *Stevenson* [1932] AC 562.
[22] *Haseldine* v. *C. A. Daw and Son Ltd.* [1941] 3 All ER 156.
[23] e.g. *Corbin on Contracts*, (1950–64), ss. 772 ff.
[24] (1861) I. 401–3.
[25] Pound (1959), IV. 280.
[26] *Arbon* v. *Anderson* [1943] 1 All ER 154 at 156.

retain possession of hire-purchase goods, by B's waiving his right.[27]

The converse view that a right implies a duty gains much of its plausibility from those instances of a right where what one has a right to is something with which another can either help or hinder. Hence arises the common thesis that to say that one has a right to so and so is to say that someone else has a duty either not to interfere with one's doing so and so or to help one to be given so and so.[28]

But, clearly, one person's right to something does not logically give rise to any duty (or obligation) in another person. Thus, my right to treat people in certain ways, such as to teach them, heal them, protect or punish them, does not impose on them a duty (or obligation) to be treated or to allow themselves to be treated in these ways by me. Still less does my right to treat animals or inanimate things in certain ways lay on them any duty to allow themselves to be so treated, for the idea of their having a duty is absurd. No one has a duty (or obligation) corresponding to my right to assume, expect, hope for, or resent something, or to complain, suggest, or query, or to condemn, sneer at, or despise someone. Rights in one person without corresponding duties in another frequently arise in games, as when one player has a right in certain circumstances to a second turn, to a throw in, to choose whether to bat or not, to tackle the man with the ball, etc. A right of a chairman to a casting vote or of a university to refuse admission to an intending student does not involve a duty in others. It is ridiculous to suppose that A's right to criticize B implies that B has a duty (or obligation) to be criticized or to listen,[29] for A may criticize B in the latter's absence or even long after he is dead. Nor is my right to pick up a stray pound note lying on the road a right against anyone and, therefore, it does not involve a duty (or obligation) on anyone to allow

---

[27] *Bowmaker Ltd.* v. *Tabor* [1941] 2 All ER 72; *Carr* v. *Broderick & Co. Ltd.* [1942] 2 All ER 441.

[28] e.g. Plamenatz (1950), 75; Olafson (1973), 174–5.

[29] e.g. Downie (1969), 123.

me to do this. I may have a right to look at my neighbour across our common fence without his having a duty (or obligation) to be looked at. Just as moral codes and commandments, like the *Decalogue*, lay down lists of duties without reference to any corresponding rights, so lists of rights, like the various bills and charters of rights, recommend series of rights without reference to any corresponding duties (or obligations). Hence, it is a mistake to argue, for example, that I cannot have a right to be let die or be killed when I am incurably ill because no one has a duty to help me to die or to refrain from interfering with my efforts to die.[30]

The situation is the same in the law. Many jurisprudents have either made the idea of a correlative duty part of the definition of a right or have alleged the existence of at least one sense of 'right' for which this holds or have supposed that one man's right at least implies another man's duty (or obligation).[31] Salmond, for instance, distinguishes the freedom of an alien to enter the country from any right to do so by the absence of any duty to allow him to enter.[32] Acceptance of the thesis that rights and duties are correlative has led some jurists to move from the definition of a tort as an infringement of a right to its definition as a breach of duty.[33] But many breaches of duty, for example not to carry offensive weapons or to aid and abet a suicide, are criminal offences, not torts.

In the cases themselves there are frequent *obiter dicta* that *right* implies *duty* and even that 'right' and 'duty' are correlative terms; as in *Quinn* v. *Leathem*,[34] *Attorney-General* v. *Adelaide Steam Ship Co.*,[35] *Howley Park Coal, etc. Co.* v. *R. & N. W. Ry.*,[36] *Lake Shore and M.S.R. Co.* v. *Kurts*,[37] all quoted in Hohfeld.[38] The court in *Broome* v. *D.P.P.* used the

---

[30] e.g. P. C. Williams (1976), 383-94.
[31] e.g. Austin, Salmond, Keeton, Kelsen, Allen, Hart, Hohfeld, Dias.
[32] (1924), 246 ff.
[33] e.g. James (1969), 3, compared with 6.
[34] [1901] AC 495 at 534 *per* Lord Lindley.
[35] [1913] AC 781 at 793 *per* Lord Parker of Waddington.
[36] [1913] AC 11, 35.
[37] [1894] 10 IND. App., 60, 37 NE 303, 304.　　　[38] op. cit. 38.

argument that Parliament could not have meant to impose a duty on anyone to stop and listen to a picket in order to prove that it had therefore not given a picket any right to stop anyone and make him listen, but only to try to persuade him to stop.[39]

On the other hand, not only might we ask by parity of reasoning what duty Parliament has, or could have, imposed on B when it gave A a right to try to persuade B to stop, but we can also point to frequent decisions that a particular right involves no duty. Thus in *Piddington* v. *Bates* the right to picket implied only a prima facie correlative duty on others not to interfere, which could cease to exist if a policeman thought a breach of the peace could possibly occur.[40] *Bradford Corporation* v. *Pickles* could possibly be interpreted as saying that the right of A to use something does not entail a duty of B not to prevent at least some of A's use of it.[41] In *Rice* v. *Connolly* it was held that a policeman's right to ask a citizen questions as to his name and address laid no duty on the citizen to answer.[42] It is accepted by the law that, for example, a right of self-defence and a right of combination give rise to no duty. Indeed, for this very reason proponents of the thesis that rights imply duties are led to deny that these are rights rather than liberties.[43]

Further, even when there is a right with a duty in the offing, the duty may not exist at the time of the right. Thus, the children of an intestate are given at the moment of his death a right to receive certain assets from the executor of his estate, though the executor's duty to hand over these assets cannot arise until the executor is, perhaps later, confirmed or appointed.[44]

---

[39] [1974] AC 587.
[40] [1960] 3 All ER 660.
[41] [1895] AC 587.
[42] [1966] 2 QB 614.
[43] e.g. Williams (1956).
[44] Cp. MacCormick (1977), 200–1 and (1976), 312–13.

(c) Conflicting rights

The assumption that in the law a right in one person logically implies a duty in another led the American jurist Hohfeld and his later followers to allege that the courts in a famous series of cases concerning trade competition and trade disputes had confused the notions of *a right*, which Hohfeldians alleged implies a duty, and *a privilege* or, as others say, *a liberty*, which they hold (correctly) does not.[45]

The issue is this. Using 'Q' as neutral between a right and a privilege (or liberty), what had been said, by Lord Lindley in Hohfeld's prime example, which he called 'the great case of *Quinn* v. *Leathem*', can be put as 'If A has a Q to earn his living in his own way, then B has a duty not to interfere with the exercise of this Q, except . . .'. Now both Hohfeldians[46] and their opponents[47] agree that the consequent of this implication, whether 'Q' be taken as a right or a privilege (liberty), was at the time, 1901, false in English law. Indeed, this consequent is still false in English law, though possibly becoming not uncommon in American law. From the falsity of the consequent it follows either that the antecedent is false or that the inference is invalid. All sides agree, correctly in my opinion, that if Q is *a privilege* (or *liberty*) then, in English law, the inference is invalid and the antecedent true. Hohfeldians, however, also argue that if Q is *a right*, then the inference is valid and the antecedent is false.

As to the alleged falsity of the antecedent, they give no evidence at all that this was or is English law or that any of the judges in the cases mentioned considered it so. It seems, on the contrary, quite clear that, whatever they meant, the courts quoted all believed that it was at the time true in English law that there existed *a right* to earn one's living in one's own way. Hohfeld himself quotes, from *Allen* v.

[45] Hohfeld (1919), 42 and ff.; Dias (1970), 256 and n. 3; Perry (1977), 41-50 and (1980). The cases are *Mogul Steamship Co.* v. *McGregor* (1899) 23 QBD 598; *Allen* v. *Flood* [1898] AC 1; *Quinn* v. *Leathem* [1901] AC 495; *Attorney-General* v. *Adelaide Steamship Co.* [1913] AC 781.
[46] e.g. Hohfeld (1919); Dias (1970); Perry (1977) and (1980).
[47] e.g. Hudson and Husak (1980).

Flood, Hawkins J. at 16 'the right freely to pursue their lawful calling' and Ashbourne LJ at 112 'a clear right to pursue their lawful calling'; also from *Mogul Steamship Co.* v. *McGregor*, Bowen LJ at 611 'the right of the defendants to carry on their business as seems best to them, provided they commit no wrong on others'; from *Quinn* v. *Leatham*, Lindley LJ at 534 'the ordinary rights of the British subject. He was at liberty to earn his living in his own way provided he did not violate . . .' and from *Attorney-General* v. *Adelaide Steamship Co.*, Lord Parker of Waddington at 793 'every member of the community is entitled to carry on any trade or business as he chooses'. Esher, MR in *Mogul Steamship Co.* at 604 said that there was up to his time a long line of cases that established 'a legal right to carry on his trade', though he quoted both authorities who spoke of a 'privilege' and those who spoke of a 'right'. In addition, the textbook writer Sir William Erle, quoted by all the judges in *Allen* v. *Flood* and by several judges in the other cases mentioned above, held that 'every person has a right under the law, as between him and his fellow subjects, to full freedom in disposing of his own labour . . .'. Apart from his assumption that the characteristics mentioned cannot be a right because that would allegedly imply the consequent, invalid in law, of a correlative duty to refrain from trade interference, Hohfeld was expressly influenced by the fact that Lord Lindley called this a 'liberty'. But to this the answer is that there can as easily be 'a right to a liberty to V' as there can be 'a right to V' itself, as in 'the right to freedom of speech or worship' and 'the right to speak or worship'. It is worth noting that Hawkins J. spoke of the 'right *freely* to pursue their lawful calling', Lord Parker of Waddington of 'the *free* exercise of his trade or business', Esher MR of the 'right to carry on his trade in a *free* course of trade' and of 'a legal right to be left *free* to· exercise his trade', Grantham J. in *Allen* v. *Flood* at 54 of the right to trade as 'a right of personal liberty', and Erle of '*full freedom* in disposing of his own labour'.

As to the alleged validity of the inference that a right implies a duty—which is our present topic—Hohfeld was able, as we saw, to quote in his support various *obiter dicta* from English and American cases, as well as from several jurisprudents. His is, indeed, the common jurisprudential view. Its falsity, however, is shown not merely by the many legal and non-legal examples I have already provided, but also by the decisions in the trade-competition cases being discussed.

Quinn v. *Leathem, Allen* v. *Flood, Mogul Steamship Co.* v. *McGregor*, and the later case of *Sorrell* v. *Smith*,[48] make it quite clear that a right of A to pursue his own business does not imply a duty of B to refrain from (lawful) interference. Even in the usual passages quoted from Lords Lindley, Bowen, Halsbury, Ashbourne, and Parker the most that is said is that the duty correlative to a right is to refrain from *unlawful* or *unjustified* interference. Fry J. in *Mogul Steamship Co.* at 625 characterized the plaintiff's right to trade as 'not an absolute right, but a qualified right—a right conditioned by the like right in the defendants', and Mathews J. in *Allen* v. *Flood* at 26 said that the right could be invaded in fair competition. Cave J., whom Hohfeld quoted with approval as carefully distinguishing a right and a liberty, as indeed he does in *Allen* v. *Flood* at 29, held at 30 and 33 that it was 'undoubted law' that a trader had a right to carry on business without disturbance except in the way of fair competition—compare North J. at 40, Lord Ashbourne at 113, Lord Shand at 166 and 173. And when Channell J. distinguished, in *Starey* v. *Graham*[49] referred to by Hohfeld, between a 'right' in the popular sense and a legal right, although he equated the former with something not forbidden by the law, he did not relate the latter to any correlative duty. Furthermore, later famous trade-dispute cases, such as *Crofter Hand Woven Harris Tweed Co Ltd* v. *Veitch*[50] and *Rookes* v. *Barnard and Others*,[51] take the same view, as

---

[48] [1925] All ER 1.
[49] [1899] I QB 406.
[50] [1942] AC 435 *per* Lord Wright at 462-6.
[51] [1962] 2 All ER 579.

does the Trade Disputes Act 1906 s. 3, which may even allow interference by unlawful acts, such as breach of contract.

In fact, what seems to have happened in regard to the *right* to carry on one's trade is that its legal protection has diminished gradually over the years in the interests of trade competition and union disputes from earlier more stringent safeguards rather than, as Hohfeldians assume, that it has become, or always was, merely a *privilege* or *liberty*. *Allen* v. *Flood* etc. are simply landmarks in this change.

(d) *Duties as protectors of rights*

Because of the existence of many examples of a right without a duty, it is a mistake to suppose that the former implies the latter. Nor is the existence of examples where both a right and a reciprocal duty are present to be explained by having recourse to two concepts of *right* or two senses of the word 'right'.[52] At most—though even this is misleading—we have two different kinds of right, namely those which are and those which are not accompanied by a duty, but not two different concepts of *right*. Often, indeed, in these cases both B's rights and A's duties arise from a common source. Thus, both B's right to repayment and A's duty to repay him arise from A's debt to B. A contract between A and B will give rise to various rights and duties in A and B.[53] But the existence of A's duty is no part of the notion of B's right. The various rights and duties of husband and wife, child and parent, employer and employee, different ranks in an institution, etc. arise not mutually from each other, but jointly from the common system in which all participate. By analogy, it is no part of the notion of A's having a father that there should be a B who has an uncle, though if A and B are first cousins, then when A has a father B will necessarily have an uncle.[54]

---

[52] As by Raphael, Downie, McCloskey, Lyons (1970), Warrender.
[53] Cp. Olivecrona (1971), 137 ff.
[54] Cp. Lyons (1970), 46–9.

Moreover, various rights and duties would be useless unless there also existed corresponding duties and rights. One person's right to be given something, for example to be protected, to be repaid, to be told the truth or to have safe working conditions, requires for its effectiveness a duty on someone else to give it and one person's right to act, for example to walk in the park, to raise an objection, or to work where he wishes, may possibly require for its exercise a duty in others not to interfere.[55]

But none of this shows any logically necessary connection between the rights and the duties themselves. By contrast, one person's right to assume, expect, or resent so and so, to feel annoyed at or proud of such and such, to complain about or query this or to sneer at or despise that requires no help or non-interference from another and, therefore, no duty to provide such.

Similarly in the law, where my right is what is often called 'a right against someone', his duty and my claim to the exercise of his duty, is not so much a logical consequent of my right as a legal protection for it.[56] In many cases it would be pointless, though not logically impossible, to give a right to A without laying a correlative duty on B. This is why jurists often suggest that A's possession of a right must involve a duty on others not to interfere with his exercise of it and suppose that a right is distinguished from a liberty by the presence of the duty of others not to interfere.[57] But even the law allows the possession of a right where no restitution for its hindrance is possible, as has occurred in, for example, the right to belong to a trade union[58] or the right to pursue a job.[59] Conversely, one person's breach of a statutory duty will usually give another person a right of

---

[55] Cp. Lamont (1946), ch. 3; Ross (1930), 48 ff.

[56] Cp. Lamont (1946), 71-3, who seems to deduce the former from the latter, Hart (1973), 179 ff. and Pound (1959), IV. 47-53.

[57] e.g. Salmond (1924), 246 ff.

[58] e.g. *Boultry* v. *Assoc. of Cinematograph Technicians* [1963] 1 All ER 716, quoted by D. Lloyd, *The Idea of Law* (Penguin Books, 1964), 314.

[59] e.g. *Davis* v. *Carew-Pole* [1956] 1 WLR 833; *Byrne* v. *Kinematograph Rentiers* [1958] 1 WLR 762, quoted by Lloyd, op. cit.

action unless there is a remedy or penalty laid down; otherwise the statute would be ineffectual.[60] But that this is not a logical implication of a right by a duty is shown by our earlier example where the Prison Authorities' breach of duty had no effect on a prisoner's rights. A good example of the protective, rather than the logical, part which a duty in one man plays in the right of another is provided by the trade competition and trade disputes earlier examined, where we saw a gradual decrease over the years in the amount of protection provided.

To suppose that there are two senses of 'right' or two concepts of *right*, one of which logically implies and the other not a correlative duty, whereas in fact there are at most rights which are legally tied to duties and rights which are not so tied is like supposing that because there are women who are legally tied to men and women who are not, therefore there are two senses of 'woman' or two concepts of *woman*, namely 'married woman' and 'spinster'. It is worth noticing that even when Bentham and Mill distinguished between duties which they held involved rights—Bentham's 'extra-regarding' duties and Mill's duties 'of perfect obligation'—and duties which they held did not—Bentham's 'self-regarding' duties and Mill's duties 'of imperfect obligation'—they, nevertheless, did not suggest that there were two senses of 'duty' or two concepts of *duty*.

To seek to explain the notion of a right by reference to that of a duty and, hence, to take the absence of a duty as proof of the absence of a right in the way that one might properly seek to explain the notion of knowledge by reference to that of truth and take the absence of the latter as proof of the absence of the former is to link up two ideas which are quite independent. Rights are rights in virtue of some title which gives them to us, whereas duties are duties in virtue of some position or authority which lays them on us and obligations are obligations in virtue of some factor

---

[60] Cp. James (1969), 248; *Cutler* v. *Wandsworth Stadium Ltd.* [1949] 1 All ER 544.

which binds us. We need no more look to the duties (or obligations) of others in order to discover our rights than to look to their rights to discover our duties (or obligations).

As I mentioned earlier, discussions and theories about the relations of rights to duties are usually not separated from discussions and theories about the relations of rights to obligations because no distinction is made between duties and obligations. Though duties and obligations are, as we have seen, different, their mistaken assimilation does not save either theory from fault, since our discussion in this chapter has, I hope, made it clear that analogous objections can usually be made to the commonly postulated theses both about the relation of rights and duties and about the relation of rights and obligations.

6

Whose Rights?

(a) Being capable of having a right

Traditional discussions of rights have usually been confined to the rights of humans. The question whether anything other than a human being could sensibly be said to have a right, let alone whether it did or ought to have such, was rarely raised. Where the law wished to extend rights to other things, such as corporations, it did so by classifying them as 'legal persons'. Despite some remarks in the eighteenth century and a few books[1] in the nineteenth century on the rights of animals and, of course, a long legal tradition— enshrined in the doctrine of Deodand—of attributing blame and inflicting punishment on animals, railway engines, bricks, etc., which caused injuries to men, it is only recently, indeed, in the sixties and seventies of this century, that much attention has seriously been given to the question whether rights can be possessed by what is not a human being. It is now debated, for example, not only whether generations of humans yet unborn, children, imbeciles, and the irremedially comatose can have rights, but also whether human foetuses and animals, plants, trees, material objects in nature, and even artistic creations in paint and sculpture can have them.

The question is usually approached by enquiring whether there are certain characteristics or a family of such characteristics which are either necessary or sufficient for the possible possession of a right. Are there certain kinds of subjects whose nature makes it logically impossible for them to have rights? Naturally, those interested in the substantial question whether such and such specific subjects, such as children, idiots, animals, or inanimate objects, can, or even do, have

[1] Lawrence (1796–8); Nicholson (1879); Salt (1892).

rights need also to enquire, as of course they do, whether such specific subjects in fact have the characteristics which, an answer to the first question holds, are either necessary or sufficient for the possible possession of rights. For example, they enquire whether, or assert that, animals have interests, are owed duties, are capable of suffering, are equal in consideration to humans, etc. Since, however, I am interested only in the nature of a right and, hence, in the characteristics of those kinds of subjects which can have rights, but not in what specific subjects do have these characteristics, I shall not discuss these latter problems.

In discussing our question certain distinctions, not always adhered to by writers on the topic, are essential. First, one must distinguish between an enquiry into the conditions necessary or sufficient for so and so to be capable of having a right and an enquiry into the conditions necessary or sufficient for so and so actually to have a right. I shall undertake this latter enquiry in the next chapter. The relation between the two enquiries is that whatever is necessary for the capability of having a right is also necessary for actually having a right, though not conversely; whereas whatever is sufficient for the capability of having a right is not necessarily sufficient for actually having a right, though the converse is so.

Secondly, one must distinguish within the first enquiry between the question whether possession of a particular characteristic (including the characteristic of being capable of having that characteristic) is a necessary or sufficient condition for being capable of having any rights at all—that is, being the kind of thing that can have rights—and the question whether possession of a particular characteristic in regard to a particular item is a necessary or sufficient condition for being capable of having a right to that particular item. For instance, the question whether A's having (or being capable of having) things in its interests is necessary or sufficient for A to be capable of having rights at all is different from the question whether its being in A's interests to V is necessary or sufficient for A to be capable of having a right to V. The relation between the two questions is that whatever is necessary for something to be capable of having rights at all is also necessary for it to be capable of having a particular right, though not conversely; whereas whatever is sufficient for it to be capable of having rights at all is not necessarily sufficient for being capable of having a particular right, though the converse is so. Thus, on the one hand, though being animate might be necessary for something to be capable both of having rights at all and of having the right to kind treatment, being rational might be necessary for it to be capable of having the right to vote, but not of having rights at all. On the other hand, though being animate might be sufficient for it to be capable of having at least some rights, it need not be sufficient for it to be capable of having the right to vote, whereas if being rational were sufficient for it to be capable of having the right to vote, it would also be sufficient for it to be capable of having at least some rights.

Despite this distinction between being capable of having rights at all—that is, being the kind of a thing that can have rights—and being capable of having a particular kind of right, it is difficult to see what conditions of substance could be suggested as either necessary or sufficient for the capacity to have rights at all which would not be one of those suggested for the capacity to have a right to a particular kind of thing. For instance, how could susceptibility to pain, the power of reason, or the capacity to take an interest in things, be either a necessary or a sufficient condition for something being capable of having rights without being necessary or sufficient for its being capable of having a right to a particular kind of thing, such as the right to be free from suffering, the right to exercise one's reasoning powers, or the right to what one was capable of having an interest in? Furthermore, any thesis that a particular characteristic is necessary or sufficient for the capacity to have a right to a particular kind of thing based on the coexistence of an instance of that characteristic and an instance of that right is disproved if other instances of the characteristic and of the right do not coexist.

As a preliminary, we should note one purely logical characteristic which is a necessary, though not a sufficient, condition for so and so's being capable of having a right, for example to V, namely that so and so should be logically capable of Ving. That this is a necessary condition is clear from the fact that that of which it makes no sense to say that it can, for example, speak, smile, marry, be fed, or be given information or that it can assume p, expect q, or feel disappointed at r cannot have a right to any of these.[2] Equally clearly it is not a sufficient condition. For, first, though the wind can blow, the roads be gritted, inflation increase, or time pass, it makes no sense to say that the wind has a right to blow, the roads to be gritted, inflation to increase, or time to pass, because the wind, the roads, inflation, or time are not the sorts of things which could have rights. Secondly, the fact that a man—that is the sort of thing which can have rights—is capable of being taller than he is, of aching all over, of being full of remorse, of deserving such and such or meaning so and so, of needing this or wanting that, does not show that he could have a right to any of these, since being taller, aching all over, etc., are not the sorts of things to which there could intelligibly be rights. Thirdly, even if A is the sort of thing which can have rights and Ving is the sort of thing to which there can be rights, the fact that A can V is not a sufficient condition for A's being capable of having a right to V. Thus, even if an animal can have some rights and being appointed a Roman consul is something to which there can be a right, nevertheless the fact that an animal can be appointed a Roman consul—as Caligula's horse was— does not prove that an animal can have a right to be so appointed. To change the example so that the chosen right

---

[2] Hobbes always insisted that one could only have a right to do what one could do, e.g. *De Cive i.* 7, 10; cp. Singer and Regan (1976), 150, where it is said that a pig cannot sensibly have a right to vote.

was one which the chosen subject could have would be to beg the question.

(b) Having an interest

One of the commonest theses about the subjects of rights is that a necessary or sufficient condition for being capable of having a right is being capable of having, or actually having, an interest; a thesis which is also assumed in the traditional view, exemplified by Ihering and Bentham—which I shall examine in the next chapter—that the actual possession of an interest is either a necessary or a sufficient condition of the actual possession of a right. This thesis is subscribed to both by some who assert and some who deny that, for example, animals or natural objects have rights, the former[3] arguing that because these are capable of having interests, they can have rights, and the latter[4] arguing that because they are incapable of having interests, they cannot have rights. Furthermore, the thesis can be taken in two ways because of an ambiguity, not always respected by holders of the thesis, in 'capable of having interests' between so and so's being of such a kind that something could be in its interest and so and so's being of such a kind that it could have (or even take) an interest in something.[5]

Clearly, something could be in the interests of so and so, although so and so could not have (or take) an interest in it or in anything. Thus, certain measures or changes could be in the interests of efficiency, peace, prosperity, the truth, or the economy, though none of these can have an interest in anything. It is even possibly arguable that something could be in the interests of an inanimate object, such as the land, one's car, or one's business, though these certainly cannot have (or take) an interest. The sorts of things in whose interests something could be are, it is plausible to say,

[3] e.g. Nelson (1956); Feinberg (1974) and (1978); Godlevitch in Godlevitch and Harris (1973); Warren (1977).
[4] e.g. McCloskey (1965).
[5] Cp. White (1975), 118–20; Regan (1976); Frey (1980).

very various. On the other hand, whatever can have (or take) an interest in anything can have something in its interests. Furthermore, only the animate—and, perhaps, only the intelligent—can have (or take) an interest. Thus, a man or his dog can have (or take) an interest in certain food or in finding certain shelter; and such food or the discovery of such shelter can be in the interests of both. The class of what can have (or take) an interest is, therefore, much smaller than the class of what can have something in its interest.

However, neither the idea of something's being in so and so's interest nor the idea of so and so's having an interest in something will serve as a criterion for whether so and so is the kind of thing which can have a right.

First, neither being capable of having nor actually having something in its interests can be *sufficient* for something's being the kind of thing that can have a right, else many things, such as efficiency, peace, prosperity, the truth, the economy, and, perhaps, the land, one's car, and one's business, would be capable of having rights.[6] And no one would want to suggest that all these can have rights. Furthermore, there are many specific things which are capable of being or actually are in so and so's interest, as when it could be, or is, in my interest to be bigger than I am or to behave diplomatically, though I could not have a right to any of these. It is, therefore, a fallacy to argue, as is commonly done, that because a certain class of thing, whether animals, the environment, foetuses, generations yet to come, as well as babies, imbeciles, etc., is capable of having, or actually has, something in its interest, therefore it is capable of having a right.[7] On the other hand, though being capable of having, or actually having, something or other in its interest might conceivably be *necessary* for being the kind of thing that can

[6] It might be objected that it cannot be inferred that because something is 'in the interests' of peace, prosperity, etc., therefore these 'have interests'. Quite so; but equally the fact that something can be in the interests of a foetus, an animal, a plant, or even a baby does not show that these have interests.

[7] e.g. Nelson (1956); Feinberg (1974); Godlevitch (1973), 158; Warren (1977), 283–4. Regan (1976) interprets Feinberg as taking 'interests' in the psychological way, but in fact Feinberg seems unclear on the matter.

have rights—a thesis for which, however, I know of no argument[8]—such a thesis would do very little to narrow the class of things which can have rights, since, as we have seen, what can have something in its interests is, arguably, very varied. Furthermore, it is not necessary that a particular item should be capable of being, or actually be, in so and so's interest for so and so to be capable of having a right to it. Even if it could not possibly be in my interests to criticize my betters, or could not even make sense to talk of its being in my interests to expect so and so, to feel disappointed or pleased at such and such, these are still things to which I could have a right.

Secondly, the capability of having (or taking) an interest in things equally fails to provide either a necessary or sufficient condition for the capability of having a right. It could not be a necessary condition if those who are incapable of having (or taking) an interest in anything at all are nevertheless capable of some rights, as when the dead have a right to a decent burial or my as yet unborn grandchildren to a share in my estate. And, of course, those who advocate the extension of rights to the inanimate, such as natural objects, or to the unintelligent, such as foetuses or even the comatose, could not accept it as a necessary condition. So and so's right to proper treatment or preservation is independent of its or his capability of having (or taking) an interest in this. More specifically, being capable of having, or actually having, an interest in a particular thing could not be a necessary condition of being capable of having a right to that. Individuals can be capable of having, and even have, rights to all sorts of things, such as higher education or a transferable vote, which for some reason, such as being children or unsophisticated adults, they are, at least at the time, incapable of having (or taking) an interest in. Even with those who are capable of having (or taking) an interest in a particular item, the possibility of their having a right to that is often quite

[8] Narveson (1977), 175, says that interests are a necessary, but not a sufficient, condition for rights. Feinberg thinks they are both necessary and sufficient.

unconnected with this capability, as when someone can have a right to what he has been promised.

Nor is being capable of having, or actually having, an interest a sufficient condition of being capable of having a right. There certainly is no such connection between particular interests and particular rights. One could be capable of having, or actually have, an interest in something, for example one's neighbour's progress, his actions or achievements, many of one's own conditions, such as one's age or size, and such things as the passing of the seasons or the rise and fall of empires, which it would make no sense to be capable of having a right to. Even when what one is capable of having, or actually has, an interest in is something one could have a right to, the former is not a sufficient condition for the latter, as where what one's actual or possible interest is in is, for example, one's actions or one's achievements. Furthermore, if being capable of having, or actually having (or taking), an interest in a particular item is not sufficient for being capable of having a right to that or some related item, it is difficult to see how it could be sufficient for being the kind of a thing that can have rights, unless it is merely a criterion for some other quality, such as intelligence, which is itself posited as a sufficient condition for being capable of having rights.

It follows from all this that no valid argument can be given either for including or for excluding, for example, children, imbeciles, foetuses, animals, natural objects, unborn generations, as holders of rights on the ground that being capable of having a right ensures or necessitates being capable either of having something in one's interest or of being interested in something. Hence, the question whether animals, natural objects, etc., can or cannot have interests, either in the sense of something's being in their interest or in the sense of their being interested in something, is irrelevant to the question whether they can have rights and need not, therefore, be decided.[9]

[9] For opposing views on this latter question, contrast McCloskey and Frey with Nelson, Regan, and Godlevitch in the works cited above.

Most of the multitude of other suggestions about the necessary or sufficient criteria for being the sort of thing which can have rights can with some plausibility be regarded as variations on either the broad idea of something's being in its interest or the narrow idea of its being interested in something.

Thus, to regard anything which is capable of having, or actually does have, a good, a benefit, an inherent value[10] or, as lawyers commonly suggest,[11] a need of protection, as being capable of having a right is similar to regarding anything whose interests can be affected as something which can have a right. And it is open to exactly the same objections, namely, that if it were a necessary criterion, it would exclude almost nothing as a possible holder of rights and, if it were sufficient, it would include many things to which no one would wish to attribute rights. In short, as a criterion for the possible possession of rights, each of these is, like the criterion of being in one's interests, too broad.

On the other hand, many criteria for the possible possession of rights consist in a narrowing, in different ways, of the suggestion that to be capable of having (or taking) an interest in something is a necessary or sufficient condition for a possible holder of a right. Such criteria range from the capability of being sentient[12] to the capability of suing in law,[13] through the capability of suffering,[14] of reasoning, of choosing,[15] of speaking a language, of making a claim,[16] of entering into a contract,[17] or of being morally conscious.[18]

[10] e.g. Regan (1979).

[11] e.g. C. Morris (1964–5); Tribe (1974); Sagoff (1974); contrast Gray (1921). Salt and Nicholson also use the need of protection as a criterion for rights.

[12] e.g. C. D. Stone (1974); Warren (1977); Linzey (1976), 26 ff.

[13] e.g. C. D. Stone (1974).

[14] e.g. Bentham, Nicholson, Regan, Singer, Warren, and Clark (1977).

[15] e.g. Hart (1955).

[16] e.g. Feinberg (1974).

[17] e.g. Grice (1974). Cp. Hobbes, who on these grounds denied rights to children, though as regards animals he seems to have argued from their inability to understand the transfer of rights to their inability to make contracts, rather than vice versa; *Leviathan*, ch. 14.

[18] e.g. Ross (1930); cp. Tooley (1972).

Many of these characteristics, such as the capability of making a contract or of suing in law, are clearly too restrictive to be necessary conditions of being the kind of thing that can have rights, though they might be necessary for the possible possession of some particular rights, such as the right to benefit from a contract or to bring an action. On the other hand, since most of these characteristics, such as the capability to sue in law, to enter into a contract, to make a claim, to speak a language, to choose, or to reason, are such that anything having any of them—and anything having any of them would seem to have most or all of them—is eligible for all, or almost all, of the attributes which, I shall later argue, logically pertain to the possessor of a right, then most of these characteristics are sufficient for being the kind of thing that can have rights, though not necessarily for being capable of having a particular right.

A variation on the first kind of 'interests criterion' which uses it to argue for the thesis that objects of art can and, indeed, do have rights, at least the right to protection from mistreatment, such as bad performance of music, trivialization of a painting, insensitive abridgement of a novel, while admitting that not all interests are sufficient for the actual or possible possession of rights, holds both that they are necessary and that certain kinds of interests are indeed sufficient.[19] But this variation is really only a version of the thesis that anything in regard to which one has an obligation has necessarily a right and, therefore, the capability of having a right, for the kind of interest which, this view holds, entails a right, is 'an obligation-generating interest'. A work of art's interest in not being mistreated is said to generate an obligation in us not to mistreat it and, hence, to give it a right not to be mistreated. To this the answer is twofold. First, the fact that something is in so and so's interest does not imply that there is any obligation to provide so and so with it. Many things may be in my interests, my country's interests, or my garden's interests, or in the interests of peace and prosperity, which

[19] e.g. Tormey (1973); contrast Goldblatt (1976).

I do not for one moment suppose anyone has an obligation to supply. Secondly, the assumption that what one has an obligation, or a duty, to do for so and so is something which so and so could have a right to, though commonly made,[20] is, as I shall now argue, mistaken.

(c) *Being beneficiary of a duty (or obligation)*

I have already discussed and disputed the more extreme, though commonly held, thesis that the existence of an obligation or a duty in one subject is either a necessary or a sufficient condition of a right in some other subject. Here our topic is the narrower thesis, not always distinguished from the extreme thesis, that a duty or obligation in one subject implies or is implied by the existence of some other subject capable of having a right.

A duty (or obligation) in one subject does not imply the existence of another subject capable of having a right. First, one can have a duty (or obligation) to do something, for example to stand to attention or to be present at certain times and places, which does not imply the existence of any other subject. Secondly, one can have a duty (or obligation) which does imply the existence of another subject, but a subject which may be either one capable of having a right or one not so capable, as when one has a duty (or obligation) to punish an offender, to polish the silver, or to sweep the lawn. Where, as above, there is a duty (or obligation) *to do* something which is not a duty (or obligation) *to* anything, then clearly, even if there exists another subject, as there need not, or one capable of a right, as also there need not, this other's capability of having a right is not implied by the first's duty. Thirdly, one can have a duty (or obligation) *to something*, which is nevertheless not capable of having a right, as when one has a duty to one's country, one's conscience or one's art. Finally, even if that to which one's duty

---

[20] e.g. by Bradley (1876), ch. v; Nelson (1956); Ritchie (1894); Lowry (1975).

(or obligation) is owed is something which could have a right, its being capable of having a right does not follow from one's having a duty (or obligation) to it. A doctor's duty to his patient not to indulge her desire for drugs does not entail that she must be capable of having a right to such non-indulgence of her desires. Hence, if a duty (or obligation) in one subject does not necessarily imply even the possibility of a right in another either in regard to whom or even to whom the duty is owed, then whether we can have duties to animals, as Bentham and Mill insisted, or only to do something for animals, as Aquinas, Kant, Whewell, Ritchie, and Rickaby argued, it would not follow, as Feinberg[21] supposes, that they must be capable of having rights.

Equally, a duty (or obligation) in one subject is not implied by, and therefore not necessary to, the existence of another subject capable of having a right. For I may be capable of having, and even actually have, a right to treat people in certain ways, for example to teach, heal, protect, or punish them, without their having a duty (or obligation) to be treated or to allow themselves to be treated in these ways. No one has a duty (or obligation) corresponding to my right, much less to my capability of having a right, to assume, expect, hope for, or resent so and so. Scholars could have a right, and many in fact do have, to criticize Plato, though he could have no duty now to be, or to allow himself to be, criticized. I can have a right to look at my neighbour across our common fence without his having any duty to be looked at. *A fortiori*, one could have a right to treat animals and both natural and artistic objects in various ways even if they cannot have duties.

(d) *Being treated rightly*

Finally, there is the common suggestion that if, and perhaps only if, so and so is something for which it is *right* for me to do such and such or for which I *ought* to do such and such,

---

[21] e.g. Feinberg (1978).

for example to provide it with this or protect it from that, then so and so is capable of having a right to that which it is right to do or which ought to be done. This suggestion is usually not distinguished from the more extreme suggestion that anything for which it is right to do such and such or for which such and such ought to be done has, *eo ipso*, actually a right to such and such, and vice versa. I shall argue against the more extreme suggestion in the next chapter.

Among those who wish to extend the notion of a right beyond the rights of human beings, some shift quite unconsciously from the position that it is right for non-humans to be treated in certain ways to the position that such non-humans can be or are the possessors of rights,[22] while others explicitly, though without any careful argument, contend that the latter position follows from the former.[23] Some, however, who sympathize with the desire to secure better treatment for non-humans recognize that it is sufficient to prove only that such treatment is something it is right to provide or which ought to be provided.[24] Others are eager to argue that non-humans can have rights because they think, possibly correctly in the current state of political thinking and the influence of the law, that to show that so and so has or could have a right to such and such is more persuasive in securing such and such treatment for it than to show merely that it is right for it to have it. Unfortunately, the fact that one conclusion has, in politics or the law, greater persuasive power than another does not show that it is correct or that it follows from that other. As a matter of fact, recent and current judicial treatment of children in English law still puts more emphasis on their welfare and interests than on their rights.[25]

---

[22] e.g. Schopenhauer; Singer (1976); Tooley (1972).

[23] e.g. Salt (1892), following Herbert Spencer; Sprigge (1979); Warren (1977); Feinberg (1976), 196; Clark (1979), 180; Auxter (1979), 221 ff. Salt betrays his unease about this implication by frequently putting 'rights' in quotes.

[24] e.g. Kant; Ritchie (1894); Hart (1955); Clark (1977); Frey (1980); Feinberg (1976); Hare (1975).

[25] See the historical discussions in Freeman (1980); though contrast *M* v. *M* [1973] 2 All ER 81 at 85 where the court said that access was a 'right' of the child rather than of the parent.

Moreover, it does not in general suggest that because they have interests they must have or be capable of having rights Equally, the law, both English and American, has been reluctant to follow the advice of some jurisprudents, such as Stone and Tribe, that natural objects in the environment should be given, or be eligible for, a legal right against mistreatment.

The fact that it is right for so and so to have such and such cannot be either a necessary or a sufficient condition for so and so's being capable of having a right to such and such— much less for its actually having a right to it—for so and so could be something for which no question of a right can arise. Its being right for me to treat books, furniture, objections, exceptions, dangers, in such and such a way is not sufficient for any of these to be capable of having a right to be treated in that way. Some books which ought to be read may even deserve to be read, but are not, therefore, capable of a right to be read. Nor is its being right for me to treat a person in such and such way necessary for him to be capable of having or even to have a right to such treatment. There are many things to which I have a right and more to which I could have a right, for example to assume this, to expect that, to punish one and reward another, which, for various reasons, it might not be right for me to do.

It is, therefore, conceptually important, however impolitic or bad strategy it may be, to keep quite distinct the question whether so and so could or does have a right to such and such and the question whether it would be or is right for it to have such and such. This is not, of course, to conclude wrongly, as some do, that there are no such things as (moral) rights or that the notion is superfluous.[26] The attribution of rights to various subjects also springs from a desire to protect their freedom. And it may be that just as some thinkers have confused rights with freedom or liberties, those who wish to extend rights to animals or nature do so because they seek to keep them free from suffering or the selfishness of humans.

[26] e.g. Frey (1980), ch. I.

But to give something a protected freedom is not, as I shall argue later, necessarily to give it a right. We can keep animals free from suffering and fields free from spoliation without having to grant them rights or the capability of having rights.[27] The legal prohibition on the shooting of various sorts of birds and animals outside restricted seasons confers protection on their freedom, but does not give them a right or assume them to be capable of one.

(e) Being a person

Most discussions about the kinds of things which can possess rights centre on the kinds of capacities either necessary or sufficient for their possible possession, whether it be interests, rationality, sentience, the ability to claim, etc. Advocates of the various capabilities are usually torn between making them so strong, for example rationality or the ability to sue, that they exclude subjects to which they wish to allow rights, whether they be children, the feeble-minded, unborn generations, etc., and making them so weak that they include almost anything, whether they be inanimate objects, artefacts, abstract conceptions etc.

I have tried to show that no criterion couched in terms of substantive characteristics is logically either sufficient or necessary in itself for the possible—or, indeed, the actual—possession of a right. What I would suggest is that such characteristics are at most a mark of a certain type of subject of which the question is whether that type of subject is logically capable of having a right. And the answer to that question depends on whether it is the sort of subject of which it makes sense to use what may be called 'the full language of rights'.

[27] English law usually denies rights to animals, e.g. Kenny, *Criminal Law* (1958 edn.), 171-2. Feinberg's (1978) allegation that the Cruelty to Animals Act 1876, ss. 2 and 3, confers rights on animals is not borne out by the language of the Act. Tribe (1974), 1342, n. 27, quotes two rather old American cases—*State* v. *Karstandiek* 49 La. 1621, 22 So. 845 (1897) and *Stephens* v. *State* 65 Miss. 329, 3 So. 458 (1887)—which do allow animals rights on the grounds that it is wrong to be cruel to them.

A right is something which can be said to be exercised, earned, enjoyed, or given, which can be claimed,[28] demanded, asserted, insisted on, secured, waived, or surrendered; there can be a right to do so and so or have such and such done for one, to be in a certain state, to have a certain feeling or adopt a certain attitude. A right is related to and contrasted with a duty, an obligation, a privilege, a power, a liability. A possible possessor of a right is, therefore, whatever can properly be spoken of in such language; that is, whatever can intelligibly, whether truly or falsely, be said to exercise, earn, etc. a right, to have a right to such logically varied things, to have duties, privileges, etc. Furthermore, as I mentioned earlier, a necessary condition of something's being capable of having a right to V is that it should be something which logically can V.

In the full language of 'a right' only a *person* can logically have a right because only a person can be the subject of such predications. Rights are not the sorts of things of which non-persons can be the subjects, however right it may be to treat them in certain ways. Nor does this, as some contend, exclude infants, children, the feeble-minded, the comatose, the dead, or generations yet unborn.[29] Any of these may be for various reasons empirically unable to fulfil the full role of a right-holder. But so long as they are persons—and it is significant that we think and speak of them as young, feeble-minded, incapacitated, dead, unborn *persons*—they are logically possible subjects of rights to whom the full language of rights can significantly, however falsely, be used. It is a misfortune, not a tautology, that these persons cannot exercise or enjoy, claim, or waive, their rights or do their duty or fulfil their obligations. The law has always linked together the notions of a person and of the bearer of rights, duties, privileges, powers, liberties, liabilities, immunities, etc., so that a change in application of one notion has

[28] The fact that a right can be claimed is no evidence for the mistaken thesis (e.g. Feinberg) that a right is a claim.

[29] e.g. Lamont (1946), 83-5.

accompanied a parallel change in application of the other.[30]
Thus, at various times in the law, gods, idols, unborn and
dead human beings, animals, inanimate things, corporations,
and governments, have been treated as persons because they
were conceived as possible subjects of such jural relations as
rights, duties, etc. who can commit or be the victims of torts
and crimes. In Roman law slaves were things, not persons,
and, hence, had no rights. The attitudes of various legal
systems to the possible rights of an unborn child depend on
how far they are regarded as legal persons.[31]

What this legal practice brings out is the importance of
using a set of concepts, for example rights, duties, privileges,
obligations, etc. together and not isolating one of them, for
example right, so that, as Wittgenstein might put it, the
lone concept is only 'idling'. The concept of a right can, of
course, be stretched—as when Trollope, for example, talks of
a house with certain grandiose features as having 'the right' to
be called a castle—and debates about the rights of foetuses,
animals, works of art, or of nature can become merely
terminological. What is important is to ask what job, if any,
is being done in such contexts by the notion of 'a right' as
contrasted with that of 'right' when it is isolated from such
normal companions as the notions of duty, obligation,
power, etc.

Something capable only of sentience or of suffering would
not necessarily be capable of exercising, owning, or enjoying
a right, much less of claiming, asserting, insisting on, or
fighting for its rights or of waiving or relinquishing them. Nor
of having obligations, duties, privileges, etc. And though it
would be capable of having something done for it or of being
in a certain state, it would not necessarily be capable of
performing tasks, assuming attitudes, or having emotions.
Hence, its possible rights, if any, would be confined to the
right to have something done for it, such as to be well treated

---

[30] Cp. Pound (1959), IV. ch. 25 and references on p. 191, n. 1.
[31] Cp. Lasok (1976); Louisell (1969); though Tooley (1972) goes too far in
making 'is a person' and 'has a moral right to life' synonymous.

or protected, or to be in a certain state, such as to be happy or free or to remain alive. Moreover, though sentience or capacity to suffer would be necessary for the possible possession of a right to anything relevant to these, such as a right to protection from suffering—because a right to V implies being logically able to V—they would not be sufficient. The fact that an animal can suffer from growing pains or a man suffer from doubt does not in itself prove that it or he is capable of a right to protection from these.

It is a misunderstanding to object to this distinction between the kinds of things which can have rights and those which cannot on the ground that it constitutes a sort of speciesism.[32] For it is not being argued that it is right to treat one species less considerately than another, but only that one species, that is, a person, can sensibly be said to exercise or waive a right, be under an obligation, have a duty, etc., whereas another cannot, however unable particular members of the former species may be to do so.

[32] e.g. Singer (1976).

7

Grounds of Rights

In the previous chapter we enquired into the characteristics necessary or sufficient for an agent or type of agent to be capable of having a right. Here our interest is in the alleged grounds of those rights which agents or types of agents capable of having a right could have or which it is variously argued they do or ought to have. The grounds to be examined are those which have been alleged to be logically—not merely morally, legally, or otherwise—either necessary or sufficient for the existence of a right and the rights are those of the kind of agent, namely a person, which everyone agrees can and does have some rights.

To have a right is necessarily to have it in virtue of something, either of some feature of one's situation or of having been given it by someone who had the right, authority or power to give it. In the latter case we can ask 'Who gave you the right to V?'; in the former, 'What gives you the right to V?'. I shall call this second question a request for the 'ground' of the right, though writers on this topic have in fact used a battery of phrases, including 'based on', 'at the root of', 'give rise to', 'springs from', 'resulting out of', etc. Before we examine the various suggested grounds, several points should be noticed. First, it is not always clear whether various writers are arguing that so and so is something which, necessarily or sufficiently, gives one a right or something which is necessary or sufficient for anything to be a right. That is, whether it is being argued, for example, that something's being in someone's interests, for his good, what he needs, or what it would be right for him to have or someone else's duty to provide, would give him a right to it or would make that a right. Though these two questions are different, I shall, because of this ambivalence in the writers, consider both types of answer together in this chapter.

A second point to note is that since writers have not always distinguished carefully between what is relevant to an agent's, or type of agent's, capability of possessing a right and what is relevant to his actually possessing a right, some repetition from the previous chapter may creep into our discussion. We can, however, cover many of the points made in that previous discussion by noting that if something is necessary for so and so even to be capable of having a right, it is even more necessary for it actually to have such a right; but the mere fact that it is sufficient for it to be capable of having a right does not show that it is sufficient for it actually to have a right.

Thirdly, we must be careful not to confuse the ground in virtue of which we have a right with the right which we have in virtue of that ground. Such a confusion underlies the supposition that we 'can identify the right as the moral role' that someone plays, for example as a parent.[1] This assimilates an answer like 'The right of a Head of Department' to an answer like 'Being Head of Department', the former of which says what right one has and the latter what gives one this right. The former, but not the latter, 'explains the right by identifying it'. Where one has a right in virtue of some experience or characteristic, for example the right to scoff at a danger which one has oneself bravely met or the right to demand trust from others because one is oneself trustful, then it is even less plausible to identify the right with that in virtue of which one has it, though one can identify it as the right of one with such experience or characteristics. *Right* behaves in this respect analogously to *reason*. Just as we can ask either 'What gives you a right . . .?' or 'By what right . . .?', so we can ask either 'What gives you a reason for thinking so and so?', or 'What reason have you for thinking so and so?' and answer, for example, either 'His past

[1] Melden (1959), 77–84; cp. Austin (1861) II. 687 ff. and Salmond (1947), s..85, that one's status is one's set of rights, etc.

behaviour' or 'The reason that he behaved similarly in the past'.

There are many kinds of grounds which philosophers and jurisprudents have from time to time alleged to be logically —not merely morally, legally, or otherwise—either necessary or sufficient for the existence of any rights.

(a) Right

One of the oldest suggestions is that the ground of rights is moral. In a general form this seems to have been the view of Grotius and Pufendorff in the seventeenth century as well as of some modern jurisprudents.[2] However, this clearly cannot be the ground of non-moral rights, whether legal, institutional, epistemological, or whatever. Though there are connections between what is legal and what is moral, there are many legal rights, such as the right to turn right on a red light in California or to abstract water percolating beneath one's land,[3] which are not based on morality, and many moral bases, such as the ingratitude or the remarks of others, which do not give anyone a legal right to do anything. Equally, institutional rights, such as that of an undergraduate to take a certain option or of a member of Senate to attend a certain meeting, need not be based on morality. Nor need the undoubted virtue of someone's present membership of a group give him any right to be a member. The right to take certain attitudes, such as the right to assume that p, to hope that q, or to expect that r is not grounded on morality. It is a mistake to say 'To call something a right (of recipience) is to say that it is morally necessary'.[4]

Even within moral rights, it is incorrect to suppose that the morality of him who has the right is a necessary ground

[2] Grotius, *De Jure Belli et Pacis* (1625) I. i. 4 'a moral quality by which a person is competent to have or do a thing justly'; Pufendorff, *De Naturae Jure et Gentium* (1672) I. 30; Phillips (1863), 6-8, 27; Allen (1931), 200; Dworkin (1977a).
[3] *Bradford Corporation* v. *Pickles* [1895] AC 587.
[4] Raphael (1967), 65.

of his right or that the morality of that to which he has a right is either a necessary or a sufficient ground of the right.

As regards the former, there are many rights, such as the right to freedom, to justice, or to life, for which the morality of the holder is not necessary, even though there can be rights, such as the right to mercy, to be trusted, or to be received back into the fold, for which his previous good character may be sufficient.

As regards the morality of that to which one has a right, it is commonly supposed that the rightness of a deed is either necessary or sufficient to give one a right to do it.[5] Indeed, the thesis is often advocated that 'to have a right to V' *means* that it is right, or at least not wrong, to V.[6] But this is a mistake, possibly based not merely on etymology, but on the fact that the idea of having a right to do something and the ideas either of someone's being right to do it or of its being the right thing to do operate in the same areas. Thus, both the notions of having a right and of being right apply not merely to the moral and the legal, but also to the logical and the factual. Furthermore, both notions are confined to what can be brought about either by or to the agent. One cannot either have the right or be right to V, where 'to V' signifies, for example, an achievement, such as to succeed, fail, discover, perceive, remember, or understand; or where it signifies a bodily or mental feeling, such as to ache or itch, to like, fancy, regret; or where it signifies a bodily or mental happening, such as to bleed, swell, or tremble, to imagine, dream, or suffer; or where it signifies to belong, need, deserve, mean, intend, etc.

Nevertheless, the ideas of having a right and of being right, whether it is someone's or something's being right, are both different and independent. It is, for example, not always right to exercise one's rights, for example to appeal

[5] Cp. MacCormick (1982), 341, 'That I have a right to do something implies at least that doing it is not wrong'; Austin (1832), 292 n., looked for a connection; cp. Dias (1970), 248; Melden (1959), 2, says 'It is trivially true that a person has the right to do what he ought to do . . .'.

[6] e.g. Raphael (1967), 56; Wringe (1981), 57, 98; Ladenson (1979), 163.

against sentence, to elect two members of similar views, to chastise one's children. Nor does it follow that, because one has in particular circumstances a right to assume, suspect, or conclude that p, therefore, it is right to assume, suspect, or conclude this. I may myself admit that it is, in certain circumstances, not right that I should have something to which I have a perfect right.[7] Conversely, there are many things which we are right to do and which are themselves right, such as helping the unfortunate or informing the authorities about something, which we would hardly claim a right to do. To say that someone was right to V, for example to insure his car or to burn the incriminating documents, is not to say or imply that he had a right to do so;[8] nor is to admit that he has a right to scoff at the danger to agree that he is right to do so. Exactly the same thing could be done by someone who had the right to do it and by someone who had no right to do it, without changing the rightness or wrongness of what was done. If I honestly and carefully, but mistakenly, thought that I had a right to V, would I not be right to do that which I had no right to do? Moreover, there are some things I may be right to do which it would hardly make sense to say I have a right to do, for example to fear or dread such and such or to forgive or remember so and so. 'It is right that I should V' is a grammatical variation on 'It is right for me to V'—just as 'It is possible, only fair, etc. that I should V' is a variation on 'It is possible, only fair, etc. for me to V'—but it is not, despite what some jurists say, a variation on 'I have a right to V'.[9]

Having a right to do something no more makes what we do right than having a reason to believe something makes what is believed to be so.[10] Equally, the fact that something is right—still more that it is not wrong—no more gives

---

[7] *Pace* Salmond (1947), s. 75.

[8] *Pace* Plamenatz (1938), 96.

[9] e.g. Salmond (1957), 262.

[10] *Pace* Raphael (1967), 207; Plamenatz (1938), 14; and even Mayo (1965), who objects to Raphael and yet allows, p. 225, an occasional idiomatic use of 'to have no right to V' as equivalent to 'to be not right to V'.

someone a right to do it than the fact that something is correct gives someone a reason to believe it. Hence, conversely, the fact that someone had no right to do so and so does not show that what he did was wrong any more than the fact that what he believed was wrong shows that he had no good reason to believe it. Because it is not illegal to do so and so, it does not follow that I have a legal right to do it any more than because something is not forbidden, it follows that it is permitted. We support the assertion that someone had the right, or had no right, to V in quite a different way from that in which we support the assertion that he was, or was not, right to V and differently again from that in which we support the assertion that what he did was right, or not right. What gives one the right to V is not what makes it right for him to V, nor is what shows how right he was to V what shows that he had the right to V. In general, someone's right to do something is a function of something present with or prior to what is done, whereas its being the right thing to do often depends on either the nature of the thing to be done or some consequence of it.[11] Whether we had any right to insure X, to refuse Y, to ask for a receipt for Z, or to burn W is quite a different and independent question from whether we were right to do any of these. I might agree that someone was right to reprove me because I was behaving badly, but deny that he had any right to do so on the ground that, for example, his own behaviour was just as bad or that he was not my mentor.

What I have a right to do, I rightfully do; whereas what I am right to do or right in doing, I rightly do. Therefore, the difference between having a right to do and being right to do or in doing shows that what I rightfully do is not the same as what I rightly do.[12] If the proposal I object to is one I believe to be wrong, then I rightly object to it—and, further, if it is indeed wrong, then what I did in objecting to it was right—but it is because I am a representative of

---

[11] Contrast Plamenatz (1938), ch. IV.
[12] Contrast Barnhart (1969), 336.

the objectors that I can rightfully object to it. Further, though anything a person could rightfully do is something he could—but not necessarily would—rightly do, much that he could rightly do, for example suppose that X is Y or decide to V, he could not rightfully do. Hence, it is a mistake to argue that because a man can be rightly described as so and so, therefore he has a right to be described in that way or that because we rightly assert what is true, therefore we have a right to assert what is true.[13] The right place for something is not necessarily its rightful place, since something could be in the right place though no question of its having a right to that place arises. Conversely, something could be in its rightful place, though that was, for various reasons, not the right place for it to be.

A further sign of the gap between *being right* and *being a right* may be their different relations to their opposites. Someone can be either right or wrong to V, but he cannot have a wrong, as he can have a right, to V. We can investigate both the rights and the wrongs of a case, but only the rights and not the wrongs of a person. Someone can be in either the right or the wrong house, but only be the rightful, and not the wrongful, owner of the house. He can rightly or wrongly decide to leave or rightly or wrongly hope that he will be allowed to stay, but he cannot wrongfully, as he can rightfully, object to an eviction order, nor, contrariwise, can he suffer rightful, as he can suffer wrongful, arrest, dismissal, or detention. In the law, 'wrongful'—as contrasted with 'wrong'—'imparts in its term the infringement of some right'.[14]

It is often suggested, particularly by jurisprudents, that 'to have a right to V' means that it is not right (or it is wrong) for anyone to interfere with or to try to prevent one Ving.[15] But such a suggestion, though superficially attractive for such rights as the right to be free, to walk in the public

---

[13] e.g. Duncan-Jones (1958), 247.

[14] *Allen* v. *Flood* [1898] AC 1 *per* Lord Watson.

[15] e.g. Bentham (1789), ch. XVI. 25, n. 1; Gewirth (1982), 2, 11, 41, 48, etc. 'necessary goods of action'.

gardens, or to receive a living wage, loses all its plausibility with, for example, the right to assume that what is not forbidden is allowed, to expect some gratitude from those we have helped, or to be indignant at one's treatment, where the idea of preventing or interfering with one's making an assumption, having an expectation or feeling so and so makes no sense.

(b) Good

A second common type of suggestion about either the necessary or the sufficient grounds of a right revolves round the idea of what is good for the holder of the supposed right. This suggestion takes various forms which, though they merge with one another even in the thought of the same proponent, need to be considered separately. Sometimes it is held in (i) the general form that a necessary and/or sufficient condition for A to have a right to V is that to V is good for him (for example MacCormick and T. H. Green), sometimes (ii) that to V is in his interest (for example the jurists Ihering, Salmond, and Pound), sometimes (iii) that to V is to his benefit (for example Bentham). I shall consider these in turn, though it is worth stressing as a preliminary point that they all make the same basic mistake as the last view, namely that of seeking the ground of one's right in the nature of that to which one has the right.

(i) For his good

The first variation is that 'having a right relates to something which in normal circumstances is deemed to be good for individuals'.[16]

Advocates of this view do not claim that this is a *sufficient* ground for something to be a right. Clearly, there are plenty of things which would be good for me, such as better health or wealth, or for everyone, such as a place in heaven, to

[16] MacCormick (1982), 338; (1977), 204 ff.; (1976); cp. Gewirth (1982).

which none of us has any right. And there are many rights,
for example to assume that p or to be indignant that q, for
which the question whether that to which one has the right
is good or bad for one seems irrelevant. There are incidentally
many things I could do for the good of others, but which
I do not really have any right to do. Sometimes this general
thesis is weakened by the admission that some rights are
not even necessarily good for the individual who has them,
while still insisting that they are of a sort which is normally
good for normal individuals.[17] What this weak version must,
I suspect, be at least maintaining is that while one can have
a right to be helped, one cannot have a right to be harmed.
But even this is dubious. It certainly is not true that if to
V would in fact harm one, for example to enter a burning
building or to eat poisoned food, then one can have no right
to do these. Nor is it true that even if V is defined in terms
of harm to the agent, then he has no right to V. I can have
a perfect right to go to Hell in my own way or to choose
what is demonstrably bad for me. Indeed, the problem for
religious believers in free will is precisely to reconcile God's
omnipotence and goodness with the right—or certainly the
liberty—He is supposed to have given his creatures to choose
their own courses of action. What, I suspect, makes the
theory under consideration sound plausible is that it is only
what is good for them that people usually seek, demand, or
claim and it is only these that others usually oppose or
defend. Hence, there arises the need of a right to these, as
contrasted with the absence of a right to what most people
do not demand and most people do not oppose, that is what
is not a good for the seeker. It may be significant that the
advocates of this theory, from Bentham onwards, were thinking mainly of rights *conferred* on people, especially by the
law, for it would certainly be strange to confer rights which
were not for the recipients' good and which they would not
seek.[18]

[17] e.g. MacCormick (1982).
[18] e.g. Bentham (1789), ch. XVI. 25, n. 1; cp. MacCormick (1977), 202 ff.

(ii) In his interests

The second variation is that either the necessary or sufficient ground of a right is an interest. Jurists, such as Ihering, Salmond, and Pound, for instance, commonly linked a right to a legally protected interest.[19] There can certainly be interests connected with one's rights, as when a road user, but not a rail user, has by statute a right against a railway company whose level-crossing gates, which are intended to protect the former's interests, contribute to an accident,[20] or where an electrocuted fireman has no statutory right of action—whether or not he has an action for negligence—against a firm, because its statutory duty is only to its employees for whose benefit the regulations were made.[21] Nevertheless, there are also, as Salmond agreed, many interests or advantages which do not give rights, for example having a fine view from one's house or protection from the weather by a neighbour's house or trees.[22] An employer's interest in keeping his men from striking does not give him any right to do so. Conversely, there can be rights not based on interests. While a beneficiary of a trust has an interest without a right, a trustee has a right without an interest. Officials of various sorts are given rights of examination, entry, etc., which may be in the interests of their masters or organizations, but are not necessarily in their own interests. The old case of *Rogers* v. *Rajendro Dutt* distinguished between what would 'prejudicially affect [someone] in some legal right' and what would 'do a man harm in his interests', only the former being 'legally wrongful'.[23]

Furthermore, to say sweepingly that 'the function of the law is to confer what is considered to be normally an advantage on a certain class by granting to each of its members a certain legal right',[24] on the one hand, fails to distinguish

[19] Ihering, *Geist des Romischen Rechts* (1871), III. ss. 60–1; Salmond (1947), s. 75; Pound (1959), IV. 53; cp. MacCormick (1977); Lamont (1946), ch. III.

[20] *Knapp* v. *Railway Executive* [1949] 2 All ER 508.

[21] *Hartley* v. *Mayo* [1954] 1 All ER 375; I QB 383.

[22] *Phipps* v. *Pears* [1964] 2 All ER 35; [1965] I QB 76.

[23] (1860) 13 Moore, PC 209.   [24] MacCormick (1977), 202.

between granting a right and granting such other advantages as powers, privileges, immunities—a failure which may be one cause of the common jurisprudential view that there are all kinds of rights, or senses of the word 'right'—and, on the other hand, tempts defenders of the interests of many subjects other than humans, such as foetuses, unborn generations, animals, objects in nature, and works of art, into speaking of their 'rights'.

Outside the law also—particularly in recent writings about the possible rights of animals—interests have been taken as the sufficient and/or necessary ground not only, as we considered in the previous chapter, of the capability of possessing rights, but of their actual or merited possession.[25] But even if we distinguish, as we did previously, between X's *having* (or *taking*) an interest in something and something's *being* in X's interest—for instance, something can be in the interests of the animate or the inanimate, but only the animate can have (or take) an interest in something—in neither case is there any logical connection between interests and rights.

First, something can be in *someone's* interests, as when being kept in ignorance of so and so or gaining access to such and such may be in your interests—and, *a fortiori*, something can be in *something's* interests, as when so and so is in the interests of peace and quiet—without its being someone's right or, *per impossibile*, something's right. It is even less plausible—and in the law would not even be suggested—to hold that the mere having (or taking) an interest in something gave one a right to it. My interest in my neighbour's wife or his ox or his ass gives me no right to them. It is an open, and frequently debated, question whether the interests, in either sense, of employees in a firm's financial accounts give them a right to access to them. Contrariwise, someone can have a right to something which it is neither in his interests to have or do nor which he is interested in doing. It may well be my right to know or

[25] e.g. Nelson (1956); Regan and Singer (1976); Feinberg (1974); Frey (1980); McCloskey (1965); cp. Passmore (1974); Wringe (1981), ch. 16.

to receive something which it is not in my interests to know
or to receive and which I am not interested in knowing or
receiving.

(iii) To his benefit

The third variation on the thesis which links a right to what
is good for the holder of the right is associated particularly
with Bentham, who argued that to have a right is to be the
beneficiary, or the intended beneficiary, of another's duty
or obligation. 'To assure (by imposing a duty on another)
individuals the possession of a certain good is to confer
a right upon them.'[26] Such a view cannot be correct if, as
I argued in a previous chapter, there can be rights without
correlative duties. More immediately, being a beneficiary is
neither necessary nor sufficient for having a right. It is not
necessary, since no question of being a beneficiary of any
one arises for the man who has the right to execute the
properly convicted, to criticize other people's work or to
assume, expect, hope, or conclude so and so. It is not
sufficient, since no question of having a right arises for the
third party who benefits from a contract between two
others, as when your family—much less your home and your
horse—benefit from my contract with you or my students
benefit from the duty imposed on me by the University to
prosecute research, or for those on whom I choose to confer
a benefit, or for sub-human creatures who benefit from
kindly treatment. As we have just seen, the beneficiary of
a trust has benefits without rights and the trustee has rights
without benefits. Even those duties that are laid on us solely
for the benefit of others do not necessarily give them any
rights.[27] Many of the duties of employees, for example to
keep records or to brighten the environment, are purely
or mainly for the benefit of an enlightened company's or

---

[26] Bowring, III, 159 ff., 181, 217 ff.; cp. Hohfeld (1919), 71, 'any sort of
legal advantage and correlated with a duty'.

[27] *Pace* Lyons (1969), 173 ff.

institution's customers or public, but they do not necessarily give those who benefit any rights. If I have a duty to see that my children do not look at more television than is good for them, do they have a right to be prevented, in their own interests, from looking at the television? Further, many legal duties, for example not to carry offensive weapons in a public place, not to murder or rape, not to misdescribe, underweigh, or, in some cases, even sell, food and drugs, though intended for the benefit of all of us, do not confer any rights on our fellows. Indeed, the idea of being a beneficiary goes strangely with the idea of having a right *to do* something—despite Bentham's attempt to explain the latter as the benefit of another's duty of non-interference—however apt it may be with the idea of having a right to *have* something *done* to or for one. Furthermore, many even of our rights to have something done for us, for example to be fed, clothed and educated, are not conferred on us, least of all by imposing duties on others, but are, perhaps, natural to us.

I conclude, therefore, that in no sense—and certainly not in any of the three considered—does the fact that something is good for someone provide a ground which is logically either necessary or sufficient for his possession of a right to it.

(c) *Need*

Nor is a *need* either a necessary or, as Hobbes, followed by several modern writers, asserted, a sufficient ground of a right.[28]

Though those who hold this view are not very careful in their expression of it, they obviously wish to restrict the relation of rights and needs to a small class of the latter, sometimes called 'basic' or 'crying' needs. But even here there is a good deal of ambiguity about the position. Sometimes

[28] e.g. Hobbes, *Leviathan*; Feinberg (1966) and (1970); Raphael (1967); cp. Vlastos (1962); Honoré (1968); Gewirth (1982), *Introduction*, who seems to move between considering this connection logical and considering it evaluative. Contrast Winslade (1971), 24–37.

it takes the extreme, but clearly mistaken, form of equating rights with such needs, either directly or via the equation of both with claims. Clearly, however, a need of food and shelter is not the same as a claim to these; and we shall see later that the very common equation of a claim to something, such as food or shelter, with a right to it is equally mistaken. More usually, it is argued that a right is 'based on' or 'arises out of' a (basic) need. Here again this is sometimes taken as a direct connection between the two, but more commonly as mediated by a connection of both to a claim. The first alternative gains whatever plausibility it has by emphasizing that the connection holds only because the need is for something valuable, such as food, shelter, life, or freedom. In other words, the right is really based not on the need itself, but on the worth of what it is a need for. That is, it is argued that one has a right to what is good for one. But this is a view we have just rejected. The second alternative relies not only on a particular thesis about the relation of a right and a claim, which we shall examine later, but on the view that a need for certain sorts of things properly gives rise to claims to them. But even if this were true, it must be objected that, first, the connection between the need and the claim would not be logical, but evaluative; secondly, it would be evaluative because of the worth of that for which there existed the need; and thirdly, and very importantly as we shall see when examining the concept of a claim, it would only show that in certain circumstances to have a need can give rise to some kind of a claim. This claim could, however, be—and, I think, is—only the claim that he who has the need for so and so (should) be given so and so. But to agree that someone (should) be given so and so is not necessarily to agree that he has a right to it.

(d) Duty

The commonest suggestion, especially among jurists, for the necessary and sufficient ground of a right is that of a correlative duty.[29] This may in part derive from Bentham's version of the 'benefit-view' just considered, according to which rights are conferred on one person by imposing on others duties and obligations to benefit him. Partly, it derives also from a common jurisprudential view that a right can be defined in terms of a duty or at the very least implies and presupposes a duty. We saw at length in a previous chapter, however, that any attempt to base one man's rights on either his own duty (or obligation) or that of another—much less to correlate it with either of these—is mistaken. We need not, therefore, repeat that refutation here.

(e) Choice

H. L. A. Hart has suggested that a necessary and sufficient condition of someone's having a right to V is that 'he should have some measure of control over the correlative obligation' or duty.[30] Such a measure of control, he argued, involves the power (i) 'to waive or extinguish the duty or leave it in existence', (ii) after a breach or threatened breach of a duty, 'he may leave it "unenforced" or may "enforce" it by suing for compensation', etc., (iii) 'he may waive or extinguish the obligation to pay compensation to which the breach gives rise'. This is part of his general view that a legal right is a 'legally respected choice', a view echoed in various forms since Hobbes's definition of 'a right' as 'that liberty which the Civil Law leaves us'.[31]

To this it may be objected, first, that some rights, such as the judge's right to pass sentence on a convicted criminal, a parent's right to punish his children, or my right to assume something or to criticize somebody, as well as my right to help or heal somebody, have, as we saw, no correlative duties and, therefore, none that could be demanded or waived.

[29] e.g. Bentham (1970), 249, n. b; Austin (1861), I. 398; Salmond (1924), 240; Allen (1931), 183-93; etc.
[30] (1973), esp. 196-201; cp. (1962), 297, 315; (1955), 180, 183.
[31] Cp. Holmes (1881), 214; Lamont (1946), 71-8; *Quinn* v. *Leathem* [1901] AC 495 at 534 *per* Lord Lindley.

Secondly, there are, especially in games, various rights which do not leave me free to waive anything at all, as when one team has the right to a throw in from the side line in soccer or rugby, as contrasted with the right which the team who wins the toss in cricket has to bat (or to put their opponents in).

Thirdly, even when there are duties correlative to my rights, it is neither necessary nor sufficient for the possession of the right that I should be able to control the duty. It is not necessary, since my right, for example, to life, to freedom, not to be grievously assaulted or maimed, to protection at work, does not carry with it any power to waive your duty not to kill, to enslave, to assault by flagellation, to maim me, or your duty to ensure my safety at work. If young children, babies, imbeciles, the comatose, etc., can have rights, these would be rights which in fact could not carry any power of waiver; and if animals, foetuses, and, *a fortiori*, inanimate objects could have rights, these would be rights which logically could not carry a power of waiver. This is not, of course, to deny that there are rights which allow me to waive any duties they may involve, as when I can exempt you from your duty not to deprive me of the property in which I have a right not to be deprived or to assault me in a boxing contest or a surgical operation, though I have a right not to be assaulted.

Such a power of waiver over the duties of others is also not a sufficient condition or ground of a right. Thus, a contract between A and B in favour of a third party may contain a provision that B has a duty to grant that favour if and only if the third party requests it; yet the third party has no right under the contract.[32]

This theory about the necessary and sufficient conditions of a right seems to assimilate the right to V to the additional right to exercise or waive that right and, hence, to insist on or waive certain common, though not necessary, consequences of the possession of the original right.

[32] Cp. MacCormick (1977), 208-9; Hart (1973), 195-6.

(f) *Claim*

Philosophers frequently, and jurisprudents almost invariably, assert some sort of logical connection between rights and claims.[33] In the next chapter I shall consider at length their various important theses. Here it is sufficient to anticipate briefly my main objections to the contention that a claim is either a necessary or a sufficient ground of a right.

Distinguishing as we should, and shall in detail later, between the *making* and the *having* of a claim and between a claim, whether made or had, that something *is* so and a claim that something (*should*) *be* so, we can see that neither the making nor the having of a claim, whether that something is or that something (should) be, is necessary or sufficient to give one a right to that to which there is a claim.

It is clear that there is no logical connection between the making or the mere existence of a claim, whether that something is or that it (should) be, and the having a right to that which is claimed. Someone may have a right to some money or to some knowledge, without claiming either that he has or (should) be given the money or the knowledge, and he may claim either that he has or (should) be given these without his having any right to them. Even to admit that someone's claim that he (*should*) *be* given some money is justified is not to admit that he has a right to it, for his claim may be justified for other reasons. The most we can say is that if he has a right to it, any claim he were to make to it would be justified. Still less is the admission that his claim that he *has* the money is justified an admission that he has any right to it.

It is almost equally clear that even the *having* of a claim, as contrasted with the *making* of it, is neither necessary nor sufficient to give a right to that to which one has a claim. This is obvious where the claim is that something *is* so. One can have various rights, for example to laugh when one

---

[33] Cp. references in ch. 8 below. Vinogradoff held that claims were the historical origin of rights.

wishes or to assume certain premises, where it scarcely makes sense to talk of having a claim that one does these. Conversely, one can have various claims, for example to fame as a philatelist or to be the inventor of a new process, where it scarcely makes sense to talk of having a right to them. Similarly where the claim is that something (should) be so. One can have a right to drink moderately or to disagree with one's superiors where the idea of having a claim to do these is very dubious. Conversely, one can have a claim to special consideration or to be treated decently for other reasons than that one has a right to them.

(g) Rules

It is often held that the existence of a rule conferring a right is the necessary and sufficient ground of the possession of that right.[34] Obviously, but unilluminatingly, such a rule is a sufficient ground. If a rule gives someone a right, then he has that right. But it does not follow, nor is it true, that it is a logically necessary ground, even though in the Law it is undoubtedly a common ground, as when the Law gives to most of its citizens over eighteen the right to vote, to partly free medical care, to sue other parties in certain circumstances, etc. But even legal rights, for example a right of way due to constant trespass or a right of competition due to a policy of private enterprise, may derive from principles or policies, rather than rules.[35] Furthermore, my right to marry whom I choose, to assume that p, to hope that q, or feel hard done by are not due to any rule conferring such rights. I suspect that the popularity of the view that all rights are due to the existence of some rule derives partly from the assumption, which I have previously questioned, that one person's rights result from another person's duties, since it is plausible to think that duties are necessarily

[34] e.g. MacCormick (1977); Llewellyn (1962), 10 ff.; Hart (1961); Flathman (1976), ch. 5; Stell (1979), 9; H. Morris (1968), 500.
[35] Cp. Dworkin (1977a), 22, 52, 90.

conferred by rules. It also derives partly from a confusion
of its incorrect thesis that all rights result from rules with
the correct thesis that rights, like all evaluative concepts, are
universalizable, so that if one person has, in certain circumstances, a right to V, then anyone else in exactly the same
circumstances must also have that right.

(h) Title

The negative conclusion of this examination of some half
a dozen of the commonest candidates for the role of a
logically necessary and/or sufficient ground of a right is that
there is nothing whose very nature conceptually gives rise to
a right. Positively, there are many diverse things which in
practice we commonly admit as possible or actual moral,
legal, institutional, conventional, epistemological, etc. grounds
of rights of various kinds. Thus, a ground of a right may be:
(i) A rule, as when the rules of pleading give the plaintiff
the right to have the contents of a will set out or the university regulations give a student the right to resit an examination. (ii) A principle, as when a murderer is denied any right
of inheritance from his victim on the principle that no one
should profit by his own wrong, though, despite the same
principle, a constant trespasser may in the course of time
gain the right of access.[36] (iii) A policy, as when a policy
of protecting automobile consumers gives them a right to
compensation for injuries received due to defects in a car
or a policy of economic efficiency gives traders the right to
undercut their competitors.[37] (iv) A licence, as when I am
given the right to fish in certain sections of a river. (v) A contract, promise, or authorization, as when in return for payment I give someone the right to use my water supply or
I authorize someone to take charge in a certain area. (vi)
Some moral situation the subject is in, as when his right is

[36] e.g. Dworkin (1977a), 23–31; cp. *Riggs* v. *Palmer* 115 NY 506. 22 NE 118
(1889). Smith (1976), ch. IX, argues that the alleged 'principle'—and the 'policy'
cited next—is really a 'rule'.

[37] e.g. Dworkin (1977a), 23–31, 90–105.

based on his needs, his desires, or his deserts. Thus, Hobbes held that if something was needed by a man to preserve his own nature, 'it followeth' that he had a right to that, while Locke said that 'The first and strongest desire . . . being that of self-preservation . . . this is the foundation of a right' to life and that the right of children to inherit 'is given' by men's 'strong desire' of 'continuing themselves in posterity'. (vii) Some deed or even suffering of the subject, as when a recent victory gives the conquerer a right, a payment gives the buyer a right, finding, inventing, occupying, or making something gives one, according to Locke,[38] a right to possession of it, my frequent help to someone gives me a right to gratitude or special consideration from him, a worker's industry while in health gives him a right to support when sick, or the unavoidable sufferings of the refugee give him a right to pity. (viii) Some antecedent behaviour on the part of others, as when your attack on my character gives me the right to attack yours, your failure to say anything to the contrary gives me the right to assume so and so, your promise gives me the right to expect such and such, your ingratitude gives me the right to feel indignant, or your debt to or loan from me gives me the right to repayment. (ix) Some characteristics of the subject, as when his capacity, his competence, his expertise, his kindness, his honesty, or his trustworthiness gives him a right to do or receive certain things. (x) The subject's position or role, as father, teacher, doctor, or husband or his identity as a human being, all of which give rise, arguably at least, to various rights connected with the qualities of such roles or such an identity.

Whether or not something can be a ground of a right depends on how it is related to that of which it is a ground. This relation, we saw, is not, for any of the usually proposed grounds, that of either a logically necessary or a logically sufficient condition. It is the same as the well-known relation between the grounds for any evaluation, whether in terms of 'right', 'good', or 'ought' and the

[38] e.g. *Two Treatises on Government*, 2nd; contrast Becker (1977), ch. 4.

evaluation itself, whether it be a logical, legal, prudential, moral, or any other kind of evalution. But one very important way in which it differs from these is that the ground of a right—as contrasted with the grounds for what is right, good, or ought to be—never depends on the characteristics of what one has a right to, but always, as we have just seen, on the characteristics either of him who has the right or of the circumstances antecedent to his possession of the right.[39] Thus, whereas to V may be something it is right or good to do or something one ought to do, because of either the nature or the consequences of Ving, neither such nature nor such consequences can give one a right to V. Indeed, as we saw earlier, the fact that to V is something it is right or good to do or something we ought to do cannot in itself imply that we have a right to V; nor vice versa. We could say—though it is not very illuminating—that whether such and such personal characteristics or such and such circumstances give someone a right to something depends on an 'internal relation' between the nature of those characteristics or those circumstances and the nature of that to which it is supposed he has the right, for example between my position as a father and my right to chastise my children, between my need of food and my right to food, between my manufacture of a tool and my right to its possession, between the logic of your argument and my right to make certain assumptions, between your knowledge or your experience and your right to venture your opinion or to criticize mine, between your behaviour and my response. Sometimes, of course—as with legal or constitutional rights or those of organized groups and games—there are explicit rules laying down these internal relations between rights and their grounds.

But on the big question, namely what exactly is the conceptual relation between something and its ground which makes the former *a right*, I have no answer except to say that

[39] Though one should not narrow the class of 'facts about those beings having rights' only to those about 'the sort of being they are', as Regan (1979), 191.

just as what *ought* to be done is what is in the circumstance
owing or appropriate, what is *obligatory* is what one *has to*
do, and what one is *at liberty* to do is what *nothing prevents*
one from doing, so what one has *a right* to do is what one *is
entitled* to, and that in virtue of which one has a right, the
ground of the right, is what entitles one. It is one's title.
But to say this is to do no more than to repeat what the
dictionary and many philosophers and jurists have often
said.[40] It is only what the interchangeability of 'having
a right' and 'being entitled' in ordinary language shows we
have all always thought.

There are, of course, all sorts of interesting and baffling
questions as to what rights, whether moral, legal, or other
wise, such and such a subject or type of subject, for example
a parent, a woman, a teacher, an employee, one who has
worked hard, is in need of so and so or has been promised
such and such, etc., has, or ought to have; and on what
grounds they have or ought to have such rights, just as
there are similar interesting and baffling questions about
what obligations and duties they have, what they ought to
do or are at liberty to do and why. But the answers to these
questions depend on various moral, legal, institutional,
conventional, etc. relationships in the complex systems to
which these persons belong. They are not purely conceptual
questions and they cannot be answered merely by knowing
what it is for something to be a right, or what it is to have
a right.

[40] e.g. Locke, 2nd Treatise, *passim*, esp. ss. 34, 51, 87, 165, 176, 180, 183,
186; McCloskey (1965) and (1979); Becker (1977), 50 *et passim*; Milne (1968),
164; Flathman (1976), 36; Wasserstrom (1964), 630; Salmond (1957), 265;
Paton (1951), 238; James (1969), 91; Marshall (1973).

8

Claims

Philosophers frequently, and jurists almost invariably, assert a necessary connection between rights and claims. Such an assertion, however, takes several different forms. Many philosophers equate a right with either a claim[1] or, at least, a justified or recognized claim;[2] and a common jurisprudential definition of a right is that it is a legally enforceable claim.[3] Some philosophers and jurists equate a claim only with one —though that the fundamental—kind of right or sense of the word 'right'.[4] Other philosophers contend merely that a right implies a claim or that a right implies a right to claim.[5]

A prerequisite to any evaluation of these different assertions is an examination of the diverse ways in which the notion of a claim is ordinarily used.

(a) Claims

The basic idea of a claim is a call (Latin *clamare*) for the acceptability of something admittedly contestable, whether it is, for example, my right to X, my ownership of Y, that so and so *is* such and such, or that so and so *be* such and

[1] Catholics as quoted by McCloskey (1965), 115; Wasserstrom (1964), 630; Melden (1977), 10, 57; Raphael (1965), 210-11; Mayo (1965), 231 ff. The *OED* gives as one definition of 'claim', 'a right or title to'.

[2] Adam Smith, *The Theory of Moral Sentiments* (1759), 'What he had a right to and could justly demand from others . . .'; Mill, *Utilitarianism*, ch. V, para. 24; Ritchie (1894), 78; Ross (1930), 50; Kaufman (1968), 605; Feinberg (1964), 642; (1966), 142; (1970), 253 ff.; and (1978).

[3] Kocourek (1927), 3; Pound (1959), IV. 69-71; J. Stone (1947), 489; Hohfeld (1919), 38 ff. and American and early British cases quoted by him at pp. 36-8; Vinogradoff (1928), 367 ff.; Hart (1962), 315.

[4] This is one formulation of Hohfeld's thesis, op. cit.

[5] 'Implies a claim': cp. Golding (1968), 530-2; 'Implies a right to claim': cp. Aiken (1968), 508; Feinberg (1966), 143.

such. This idea takes three different forms, which are, however, not due to, nor do they imply, different senses of the word 'claim', but syntactically different constructions which explain different implications and different characteristics.[6] These I shall dub the 'indicative' use, the 'subjunctive' use, and the 'possessive' use.[7]

(i) The indicative use

An indicative claim is a call for acceptability of the supposed fact that so and so *is* the case, just as an allegation is a dubitable assertion that it is, or a suggestion a tentative proposal that it is. And to make such a claim, that is, to claim, is to assert in this fashion that so and so is the case, just as to make an allegation or to allege, and to make a suggestion or to suggest, is to assert in these other fashions.

An indicative claim *that* so and so *is* the case can sometimes also be advanced either by claiming (making a claim) *to V* or claiming (making a claim to) *X*, where '*V*' stands for a verb and '*X*' for a noun phrase,[8] just as to expect or hope *that* someone *will depart* is to expect or hope for him *to depart*, or to expect or hope for *his departure*; and to promise or arrange *that* you *will return* is to promise or arrange *to return*, or to promise or arrange *your return*. Thus, to claim, or a claim, to use a pint of oil per 100 miles, to have climbed Mount Everest, to be heir to the estate, to be or have been victimized, to know the names of the Kings of England, or to be full of remorse for one's deeds, is to claim, or a claim, that these things are so. Similarly, to claim, or a claim to, an ability, a power, some knowledge or complete ignorance of the matter, several advantages for one's

[6] *Pace* Feinberg (1970), 251-2.

[7] These are quite different distinctions from those of Feinberg (1970) which I did not come across until I had finished this essay. I have added footnotes to show where I disagree with his analysis.

[8] Feinberg (1970), 250, separates 'making a claim to' from 'claiming that' because he wrongly confines the former to legal claiming and to making claim to something as a right. But one can make (some, any, no) claim to originality, perfection or infallibility or to be original, perfect, or infallible.

invention, 80 per cent accuracy in one's forecasting, a hit or other success, is to claim, or a claim, that this is the case. To disclaim any of these is to deny them.

Indicative claims, whether made or not,[9] can be weak or strong, wide or limited, dubious or plausible, clear or confused, wise or rash, examined or tested and, most importantly, they can be true or false, proved or disproved, confirmed or unconfirmed, supported or unsupported by evidence.

(ii) The subjunctive use

A subjunctive claim is a call for acceptability of the proposal that something (*should*) *be* the case; it is a call *for* it, a request or demand for it.[10] Such a claim can—in ways parallel to an indicative claim—sometimes also be expressed either as a claim *to V* or *to be Ved* or a claim *to X* or *for X*, just as a request or demand is a request or demand *to V, to be Ved,* or *for X*. And to make such a claim is to claim to *V* or to be *Ved* or to claim *X*, just as to make such a request or demand is to request or demand to *V* or be *Ved* or to request or demand *X*. Thus, a claim to take 50 per cent of the profits or to go first, to be fed properly or to be told what happened, to protection, immunity, a fair hearing, one's attention or compassion, is a claim, request, or demand, for these things to be, or that they (should) be, the case. Similarly, a claim *for* expenses or a new carpet, *on* someone's time or on the family estate, is a claim that one (should) have these things. Conversely, one can disclaim what has been left to one in a will.

Subjunctive claims, unlike indicative claims, are not true or false; they are not confirmed or unconfirmed, proved or disproved, made out or not made out. Nor are they supported or refuted by evidence. They are just or unjust,

---

[9] *Pace* Melden (1959), 13. Unmade claims can be examined as easily as, e.g., unmade allegations or suggestions.

[10] Adam Smith uses 'demand'.

legitimate or illegitimate. They are supported by reasons. They are granted, turned down, or refused. One can subjunctively, but not indicatively, claim something *as* a reward or a recompense, as one's due or as a favour, as damages or expenses, as a privilege or a right. Subjunctive, but not indicative, claims can be made against others; such a claim can be the first, or a prior, claim on something or somebody. Commonly we claim, indicatively, to have what we think we have—whether it be knowledge, an advantage or success—but, subjunctively, to have or be given what we think we do not already have—whether it be protection, attention, or fair treatment—just as we commonly assert what we think to be so, but ask for what we think we do not have. We can, however, claim indicatively that we will have what we know we do not yet have and subjunctively that we should have what we know we already have, if the legitimacy of our possession of it is being contested.

When either indicative or subjunctive claims are expressed grammatically as claims *to V*, or *be Ved*, and as claims *to* some *X*, often only the context or the nature of what is claimed will make it clear which claim is being made. Thus, a claim to know what happened could be either a claim that one does know, or a claim that one (should) be allowed to know; a claim to be fed only bread and water is likely to be a claim that one is being fed only these, whereas a claim to be fed decently is likely to be a claim that we (should) be fed decently. To claim a share in the work that made the company successful is probably a claim that one did have such a share, whereas to claim a share in the profits is more likely to claim that one (should) have such a share. To claim immunity from prosecution, exemption from tax, or the privilege of bringing in a measure, could be to claim either that this is the case or that it (should) be the case.

This contrast between what I have called the 'indicative' and the 'subjunctive' use of a concept, and also the syntactical ambiguity to which it gives rise, occurs with other philosophically important concepts. Take *ought*, *must*, and *reason*. There is an ambiguity in the remark that the teachers *ought* to get a rise in salary, between the reasonable prediction that this will happen, since it has been agreed by Parliament, and the reasonable prescription that it should happen, since they have such a demanding job. There is a similar ambiguity in the remark that the Opposition *must* be bold, between the suggestion that this is the only explanation of their success in having stopped a measure and the advice that this is their only way to stop it. Similarly, a *reason* for disliking something can be either a reason why one does dislike it or a reason why one should dislike it.

D. N. MacCormick has recently suggested that there is a third type of claim, which he calls a 'claim expressed by an imperative', for example 'Give me the hundred pounds you owe me', additional to 'indicative' and 'subjunctive' claims and which he argues provides a specific relationship between rights and claims.[11] This 'imperative' claim is not, I think, different from, but only a way of expressing in direct speech, what I have called a 'subjunctive' claim.

First, its difference is not shown by any 'clear difference' between 'claim' followed by a noun (MacCormick's examples are £100, civilized treatment, reward, £5, damages, a money sum, an injunction, specific performance, a declaration, a remedy) and 'claim' followed by an indicative clause or 'claim' followed by a subjunctive clause. For both the indicative claims and the subjunctive claims can, as we saw, be expressed by 'claim' followed by a noun, for example claiming an ability, advantages, ignorance, or claiming protection, immunity, a fair hearing. The use of a noun form for the subjunctive is, indeed, common with many other verbs than 'claim'. Thus, one can demand or require £100 or that one be given £100; one can advise a return to work or that there be a return to work.

Secondly, its difference is not clearly shown by its mood. For the reported speech form of an imperative claim is expressible either, like subjunctive claims, in the subjunctive—

[11] (1982).

MacCormick's examples are the claims 'that he make repara tion', 'that the court order be the appropriate remedy' 'that one's rights be recognized'—or, like both subjunctive and indicative claims, in the infinitive—for example the claim 'to be treated in a civilised manner'.

Thirdly, its difference is not shown in legal 'statements of claim'. MacCormick explains that such a statement consists of a list of allegations of the material facts and a claim for a remedy. But the former of these are our familiar indicative claims, for example the landlord's claim that he had given the tenant notice or the employee's claim that he was dismissed without notice. And the latter, which in the words of MacCormick's 'set formula' are expressed by 'claim' followed by a noun, for example 'claim damages, an injunction or a declaration', are, I submit, subjunctive claims that the plaintiff (should) be given these.

Fourthly, its difference is not shown by stressing, as MacCormick does, that it is a 'species of demand', for a subjunctive claim can, I argued, be likened to a 'call for, request or demand'.

What the existence of claims expressible in direct speech by the imperative does bring out—and what I was confused about in the paper on which MacCormick was commenting —is that there is a difference not only between claiming that X *is* Y and claiming that X *be* Y, but also between claiming that X *be* Y and claiming that X *ought to be* Y— both of which can be expressed as 'X *should be* Y'. This is clear from the fact that whereas one can claim that X ought to have been Y as one can claim that X was Y, there is no past tense claim corresponding to the claim that X be Y.

I shall argue later that 'imperative claims', whether or not they are a third type, are related in the same way as subjunctive claims to rights.

(iii) The possessive use

This is not a kind of claim, or a kind of claiming, additional
to the indicative and subjunctive. It is a peculiarity about the
notion of 'having a claim', whether the claim is indicative or
subjunctive, or ambiguous between the two. The peculiarity
is that, though indicative claims can be either true or false,
and subjunctive claims can be either justified or unjustified,
the phrase 'to have a claim'—as well as 'to have some,
a slight, a good, a certain claim'—seems to imply that the
claim is, prima facie at least, either true or justified. Though
someone can *make* a false or unjustified claim, he cannot be
said to *have* a false or unjustified claim.[12] To admit that he
has a claim, whether indicatively to be the first man to have
climbed Mount Everest or to a longer acquaintance with
the President than any other man, or subjunctively to be
given preferential treatment or to mercy, or ambiguously
to a share in the money, is to admit that there is at least
some substance in his claim even if it is not conclusive.
In a similar way, to say that he *can* claim so and so is to say
that he can fairly, properly, rightly claim it. In this respect
'to have a claim' is like 'to have a point, an argument, a case'.
Though one can 'put' a point, an argument or a case which
is invalid, one cannot 'have' a point, an argument or a case
unless there is at least something in it.

Though, as we shall see, philosophers and jurists who
conceptually link claims and rights move around confusingly
and confusedly between the indicative and subjunctive and
the possessive and non-possessive use of 'claim', the possess-
sive use is the most relevant. It is, therefore, important to
show that the existence or the making of either an indicative
or a subjunctive claim neither implies nor is implied by the
having of a claim.

I do not have to have a claim in order to make one; nor do

---

[12] Feinberg's denial of this (1970), 253 on the ground that 'if it is not redun-
dant to pronounce another's claim valid, there must be such a thing as having
a claim that is not valid' confuses the correct 'A's claim is invalid' and the incorrect 'A has an invalid claim'.

I have to make one in order to have one. One can claim either that so and so *is* the case, as when one claims to be innocent or to have been assaulted, or claims a certain skill or some experience, or that so and so (*should*) *be* the case, as when one claims to be heard or claims shelter; but if these claims have no substance, then one has no claim to any of these things. Only a small number of those who make competing claims on someone's time may have any claim to that time. Indeed, often when one makes a claim, true or false, to something, for example to ache all over or to be full of remorse, it is not clear what sense it would have to ask whether one has a claim to this; and one can, of course, claim, truly or falsely, that one has a claim. Conversely, one can have a claim, whether it is a claim to be the discoverer of a new process or to be treated honourably or a claim to fame or to fair treatment, which, for various reasons, neither he nor anyone else has ever made on his behalf.[13] Because there is no necessary connection between making a claim of any kind and having one, the inarticulate, the ignorant, or the unconfident are, in this respect, at no disadvantage compared to the more advanced. Children and animals can have claims to possess qualities and to receive treatment despite their inability to make any such claims.

This is not to deny that if the claim one makes has substance then—provided this makes sense—one has a claim; and, conversely, if one has a claim to something, then any claim to it which one were to make would have substance. But, of course, this truism is no different from a host of others which have nothing to do with claims. Thus, if the point one makes, the explanation one gives, the solution one suggests, the argument one advances, or the case one argues has substance, then one has a point, an explanation, a solution, an argument, or a case; and conversely, if one has a point, an explanation, a solution, an argument, or a case, then any such which one were to advance would have substance.

[13] Cp. cases quoted by Dias (1970), 243, n. 1; Golding (1968), 530, 544, 549; Melden (1959), 13–15.

Furthermore, just as one can put forward an objection, an explanation, a solution, a point, a case, or an argument without 'having' one, because to put forward any of these is to put forward something *as* one, which it, unfortunately, may not be, so to put forward a claim is to put forward something *as* a claim, which one can do without 'having' any claim. And just as what someone puts forward in these other instances is called 'his' objection, explanation, case, etc., so the claim he makes is his claim. Hence, paradoxically, so and so can be 'someone's' claim, though he 'has' no claim, just as such and such can be 'someone's' explanation, solution, point, or case though he 'has' no explanation, solution, point, or case.

The notion of a claim is used in the law in exactly the three ways in which, I have suggested, it occurs in everyday thought and language. First, the landlord who claims that he had given the tenant notice,[14] the woman graduate who claims that she is entitled to vote,[15] Parliament which claims jurisdiction over all that happens in the House, a body which claims that a power has been conferred on it by law, the trader who claims for breach of contract, the employee who claims wrongful dismissal, a spouse who claims that the furniture in the matrimonial home is hers,[16] and the plaintiff who claims that he is the owner of the goods, are all claiming indicatively that so and so is the case. Secondly, to claim or disclaim a gift in a will,[17] to claim a patent for an invention,[18] to claim something under an insurance policy,[19] to claim to levy taxation without consent of Parliament, to claim a special prerogative, and, more obviously, to claim that one's

[14] Cp. cases given in *Woodfall on Landlord and Tenant*, 26th edn. (1960) I. ch. 18, s. 7.

[15] *Nairn* v. *University of St. Andrews* [1909] AC 147.

[16] Cole (A bankrupt), *Re, Ex parte The Trustee* v. *Cole*, [1963] 3 All ER 433, and cases given in P. R. H. Webb and H. K. Bevan, *Source Book of Family Law* (1964), ch. 16.

[17] W. J. Williams, *The Law Relating to Wills*, 3rd edn. (1967), ch. 37.

[18] T. A. Blanco White, *Patents for Inventions and the Protection of Industrial Designs*, 4th edn. (1974), ch. 2.

[19] Cp. *MacGillivray and Parkington on Insurance Law*, 7th edn. (1981).

husband pay one a sum of money or that others not interfere with one's business, is to claim subjunctively that one (should) be given what one claims. All such claims, whether indicative or subjunctive, can be stated, made, entered, advanced, proved, made good, satisfied, met, maintained, enforced, registered, disputed, rejected, fail. One can in these ways be entitled, or have a right, to claim, for example, a writ of delivery, or, conversely, claim to be entitled or to have a right, for example, to compensation, to a car, or to judgement in a case. Finally, to hold that a claim to a patent is valid, that a claim to the whole of a debt has been established, that an insured has proved his claim, or that a subject has maintained his claim against the Crown for compensation, is to allow in all these cases that the plaintiff has a claim.

(b) Claims and rights

Having sketched out the various uses of the notion of a claim, I want now to examine their relations to rights. And this in two ways. First, to show briefly that though rights are something which can be claimed, whether indicatively or subjunctively (or, if this is different, imperatively), possessively, or not possessively, they are claimed in exactly the same way as any of the countless other things which we have seen can be the subject of claims. Secondly, to investigate how the idea of a right to something is related to the idea of a claim to the same thing.

(i) The claiming of rights

One can indicatively claim possession of a right to something, whether by claiming that one has the right to it, or that it is one's right, or by claiming the right to it. Thus, the House of Lords may claim to have the right to hold up legislation which is not popularly supported, a head of a department might claim that to have one secretary for every ten members

of his department is his right, and the management may claim
the right to refuse admission to whoever it pleases. Claiming possession of a right is, however, no different from
claiming possession of anything else, whether it is knowledge,
experience or an umbrella, by claiming that one has it or that
it is one's own or simply by claiming it. And just as neither
claiming to have anything else implies that one does have it
nor does having it imply making any claim to have it, so
claiming to have a right neither implies, nor is implied by,
having a right. It is just as mistaken to say 'that a right
should exist, it must be *claimed* . . . in other words the
subject must assert something as his right'[20] as to assume—
as philosophers who make the conviction that one knows
a necessary condition of knowing sometimes seem to do—
that 'for knowledge to exist, it must be claimed . . . in other
words the subject must assert something as his knowledge'.
The former would be too quick a way to deprive children
and—as does Ross[21]—animals of their possible rights, just
as the latter would be too quick a denial of knowledge to
the unconfident. Of course, if the claim to a right were true,
it would imply that the claimant had the right, and, conversely, if the claimant has a certain right, then any claim
he made to it would be true. But this holds for a claim to
possession of anything whatsoever. Further, since the fact
that someone who had something would be undoubtedly
right in claiming that he had it does not in general provide
any reason for supposing that he would have a right to
claim that he had it, it is difficult to see why 'for every right,
there is a further right to claim, in appropriate circumstances,
that one has that right'.[22] *Rightly* claiming to have what one

[20] Vinogradoff (1928), 367-8; cp. Cranston (1973), 81; Melden (1959), 14.
Feinberg's 1970 view that a claim is an 'assertion of right' would allow no sense
to 'having a claim'—to which he rightly does allow sense—since this would
then be the senseless 'having an assertion of right'.
[21] (1930); cp. Narveson (1977), 161-78. See Feinberg (1976), 190-6, who
allows that animals can have rights because others can make claims on their
behalf; cp. McCloskey (1965).
[22] Feinberg (1966), 143.

does have is not the same as *rightfully* claiming to have what one does have.

Similarly one can subjunctively (or imperatively) claim that one (should) have a right to something, whether by claiming it as a right or by claiming a right to it. Thus, one may claim certain goods as a right in contrast to claiming them as a reward, as expenses, or as one's due; one may claim for one's self the rights of any citizen or those of a husband; one may claim the right to something, whether to property or protection, to go or to be accepted, to know or to feel annoyed, or one may simply claim one's rights as one might claim one's wages. Once again, however, a claim that one (should) have or be given a certain right is no different in kind from a claim that one (should) have anything else. Certainly, to claim the right to protection, a fair hearing, damages, one's audience's attention, or the right to be treated properly or be fed decently, is to claim something different from what one claims when one claims protection, damages, to be fed properly, etc., themselves, just as to vote, to fight, or to die for the right to freedom, money, or a change of party is to vote, fight, or die for something different from freedom, money, or a change of party themselves. But claims for different kinds of things are no more different kinds of claims than votes or fights for different kinds of things are different kinds of votes or fights.

There is no closer logical connection between a subjunctive (or imperative) claim that one (should) possess a particular right and the actual possession of that right than between an indicative claim that one does have it and the actual possession of it. Not only can a claim that one (should) have a right as easily—though on different kinds of grounds —be disallowed as a claim that one does have it can be disproved; we saw that sincerely to claim that one (should) have something, whether a right or anything else, often suggests, though it does not imply, that one thinks that one does not already have it. In short, it is simply a fallacy to assimilate, as many jurists seem to do, a 'right' and a 'claim of right'.[23]

One source of the fallacy that a right is a claim may be that in *saying* 'I have a right *to V*' I am making a claim. But equally in *saying* 'I know that *p*' or 'I own *X*' I am making a claim; yet neither knowledge nor ownership is a claim. What we claim, that is the thing claimed, in making a claim to a right, is not itself a claim, any more than what we claim in making a claim to knowledge or ownership is itself a claim.[24] Underlying this source of the fallacy is a confusion between the meaning of 'having a right' and the illocutionary force of saying that one has a right—which is alleged to be making a claim on others. This confusion is worse confounded when a distinction between invoking one's rights in order to make demands on others and invoking them as a response to a demand to justify oneself is thought of as a distinction between two kinds of rights, namely claim-rights and justification-rights, the former of which implies, while the latter does not, duties in others.[25]

Finally in this section, we should note that the syntactical ambiguity in the remark that someone is claiming something, for example an exemption or a privilege or to be fed, as between claiming that one does have and that one (should) have this, infects claims to rights. Though the manager who claims the right to refuse admission to a drunk is probably claiming that he does have this right, and the parent who claims the right to send his children to a school of his choice is probably claiming that he should have this right, a chairman who claims the right to veto, and the political group who claim the right to picket may be making either an indicative or subjunctive claim. Claims to legal rights are

[23] e.g. Wasserstrom (1964), 630; Dworkin (1977a), 146, 199, 269. A 'claim of right' as a term of art, e.g. in the Larceny Act 1916, is really an honest claim (or belief) that one has a right; cp. Williams (1961), ss. 107-17; *R.* v. *Bernhard* [1938] 2 KB 264.

[24] Feinberg (1970), 251, argues that claiming is 'essential to the very notion of right'; but equally plausibly or implausibly we might argue that claiming is essential to the notion of ownership.

[25] e.g. Ladenson (1979).

usually indicative, though claims to, for example, possession of a child may be subjunctive. Claims to political rights, as contrasted with political declarations of rights, are usually subjunctive.

(ii) A claim to and a right to

The second important question about the relations of rights to claims is whether either the making, the existence or the possession of a claim, whether indicative or subjunctive (or imperative), to something implies, is implied by, or is equivalent to, the having of a right to the same thing.

Clearly, there is no logical connection between making a claim, whether indicative or subjunctive (or imperative), and having a right to that which is claimed. For first, one may have a right to something which one has not claimed, either indicatively or subjunctively (or imperatively), at all. I may have a right to some money or a right to know a name, though I don't indicatively claim the money or to know the name, either because I don't think I have the money or the knowledge or because I know I haven't. Or I may have a right to be given something, whether money, protection, or freedom, for which I make no subjunctive (or imperative) claim because I have no desire for it. Secondly, one may claim something, either indicatively or subjunctively, to which one has no right. Thus, I may claim to have some money or to be surprised at something, though I have no right to the money or to be so surprised. Or I may claim that I (should) be given some protection, immunity or goods which I have no right to have. Indeed, my claim that I have or do so and so may be proved and my claim that I (should) have or be given such and such may be granted, without its being proved or granted that I have or be given rights in respect to so and so and such and such. To uphold my claim to be the long-lost heir to the estate is to admit that I am the heir, not that I have a right to be the heir, even though being the heir gives me a right to the estate. To admit my claim to the authorship of the document is not to admit any supposed right to be the author. And granting my claim, like granting my request or demand, to be given protection or immunity is granting that I (should) be given them, not that I (should) be given a right to them. Not even rightly claiming, much less merely claiming, something gives one a right to it. Hence, taken at their face value, common philosophical and juristic analyses of *rights* as 'legally enforceable claims', as 'recognised' (Ritchie), 'inviolable' (Catholic writers quoted by McCloskey), 'strong' (Wasserstrom), or 'valid' (Feinberg) claims, are confusions between 'rightly claiming' something and 'having a right' to it. It is simply a mistake to assert that 'we mean by a right something that can be justly claimed'.[26] Thirdly, not only is it often false to say that that which I claim I have a right to or that which I have a right to I claim; but, in indicative claims at least, it sometimes does not even make sense to talk of having a right to some of the things which one can claim, for one can claim almost anything. Thus, I can claim—even rightly claim— but not have a right, to be able to do so and so, to need such and such, to intend this or that, to ache all over, or to be full of remorse, to be of such and such a size, age, colour, etc. This shows itself also in the syntactical feature of English that, whereas a claim to V or be Ved is, when the claim is indicative, a claim that one *does* V or *is* Ved, a right to V or be Ved cannot be a right that one *does* V or *is* Ved, but only a right that one V or *be* Ved (or that one *should* V or *be* Ved).

It might be, however, that philosophical and juristic analyses of rights in terms of claims are intended to equate 'having a right' not with 'rightly claiming', but with 'having a claim', that is, with what I have called the 'possessive' use of the notion of a claim.[27] Let us, therefore, conclude with an examination of the relations between having a right to something and having a claim to it.

[26] Ross (1930); cp. 'justly demand' (Adam Smith).
[27] e.g. Wasserstrom (1964); Feinberg (1964, 1966), etc.

It is, independently, clear that having an indicative claim to something neither implies nor is implied by having a right to it. The former does not imply the latter, since one may have, for example, some claim to fame as a philatelist or to be the inventor of such and such a process without our being able to say, either truly or sensibly, that he has a right to fame as a philatelist or a right to be the inventor of such and such a process. Nor is having a claim implied by having a right, since one can have various rights, for example to laugh when one likes or to assume certain premisses, without its even making sense to talk of having an indicative claim to do these.

It is also clear that having a subjunctive (or imperative) claim, for example to special consideration or to be treated decently, does not imply having a right to them, for one's possession of a claim may be based on other considerations, such as the justice of such treatment.[28] To suppose otherwise is to confuse what it is only right for one to have—or right that one (should) have—with what one has a right to have— or a right that one (should) have. It may be (only) right for me to sacrifice myself for another without its being my right to make such a sacrifice, while the fact that I have a right to chastise my son may not make it right for me to do so. One can ask whether someone has a rightful claim to such attention, or by what right he claims such authority. The question can arise whether, for example, one immigrant has a stronger claim than another to entry to this country, even though neither has a right of entry. Nor, conversely, is having a subjunctive claim to something implied by having a right to it, as when someone has a right to special consideration, to be treated decently, to go where he wishes. Having a right to something is usually a, though not the only kind of, reason for possession of one's claim to it or to something else.[29] Furthermore, many of the things one can have a right

[28] MacCormick (1982) usually holds that an 'imperative claim' implies a right, though sometimes that it implies only 'some general ground'.
[29] Melden (1959), 17; MacCormick (1982) holds that 'having rights entails having justified (imperative) claims'.

to are things to which it makes rather dubious sense to speak
of having a claim. We can certainly have a right to, but rather
dubiously have a claim to, do or say what we like, to inspect
and make copies of certain documents, to make, in California,
a right turn against a red light, to drink moderately, to
marry—or to advise, disagree, beg, begin, kill, choose,
conclude, laugh, promise, prevent, etc.—to assume so and so
or to expect such and such, or to feel certain things, such as
badly done by or indignant or jealous; or a right to a second
chance, or one's own opinion.

It is significant that analyses of rights in terms of claims
usually go hand in hand with an emphasis either on rights to
property or, as jurisprudents unidiomatically phrase it, on
rights 'against' people, both of which are rights to have something done to one, rather than a right to do anything, and
therefore exist in areas where the idea of a claim to something, like the idea of a request or demand for it, is appropriate.[30] Thus, Kocourek says that a right 'in the strict
sense' is a 'capability to claim an act from another', whether
this be *in personam* or *in rem.*[31] Such a view is fostered by
the assumption that where one person has a right, someone
else has a duty whose performance one can demand or claim
and to which one has a claim. Hence, followers of Hohfeld
call some rights 'claim-rights';[32] Hohfeld himself suggested
'claim' as one sense, the strict sense, of 'right' and quoted
some early American and Scottish court *obiter dicta* in
support of this suggestion.[33] Where there is no correlative
duty and, hence, no claim against another, he thought,
wrongly as I shall argue in chapter 11, that the so-called
'right' was really a 'privilege' or 'liberty'. Similarly, philosophers sometimes introduce two senses of 'right', namely

[30] Cp. Feinberg (1966), 137 ff.; (1964), 642; Lyons (1969), 174.
[31] (1927), 3; Pound (1959), IV. 56, 69-71.
[32] Hohfeld (1919); cp. Dias (1970); Dworkin (1977a); MacCormick (1977),
189-209; Feinberg (1970), 249.
[33] e.g. *United States* v. *Patrick* (1893) 54 Fed. Rep., 338, 348 *per* Jackson, J.;
Lonas v. *State* (1871) 3 Heisk. (Tenn.) 287, 306-7 *per* Sneed J.; *Mellinger* v.
City of Houston (1887), 68 Tex., 45, 3 SW, 249, 253 *per* Stayton J.; *Studd*
v. *Cook* (1883) 8 App. Cas., at 597 *per* Lord Watson.

that in the 'right to act' and that in the 'right to receive'; the latter of which is then analysed as a 'claim on another'.[34] At other times, even the right to act is analysed as a claim on others, for example as a claim to their non-interference.[35] But, apart from its own implausibility, a division of two senses of 'right' leaves unexplained such rights as the right to assume or expect that p, the right to feel pleased with oneself or the right to feel indignant, which are rights neither to act nor to receive. Sometimes, the further step is taken of denying that there is, strictly speaking, such a thing at all as a right *to act*; there is, it is said, only a 'liberty' to act.[36]

We have, however, seen in detail in an earlier chapter that the assumption, so common among philosophers and jurisprudents, that rights imply duties is mistaken. One cannot, therefore, argue that a right in one person logically implies a claim that an allegedly accompanying duty in another person be performed, though often such a duty may, in the law at least, exist as a protection and, as such, be legally due.

I conclude that having a right to something and having a claim to it are not mutually implicative nor, therefore, equivalent notions. Much less are rights and claims themselves—even true or justified claims—the same. As we have seen, rights, but not claims, can be given, conferred, taken away, earned, enjoyed, or exercised; while claims, but not rights, can be made, advanced, laid, made out, settled, allowed, met, or rejected.

---

[34] Raphael (1962), 348; cp. Raphael (1967), 102-5; Downie (1969), 116-26; Arnold (1978), 77.

[35] e.g. Pollock (1961), 33, 46-7; Lamont (1946), ch. 3; Ross (1930), 48 ff.

[36] Raphael and Downie (see n. 34 above); Kocourek (1927), 3; Williams (1956), 1129-50. Mayo (1965), 225, holds that the so-called 'right to act' means only 'it is right to act', while Raphael and Downie say it means 'it is not wrong to act'.

9

Liberties

There is a tradition going back at least to Hobbes and Spinoza which equates a right with a liberty and the idea of having a right to V with the idea of being free to V.[1] This tradition is preserved by those jurisprudents and philosophers who hold that 'liberty' is at least one sense of 'right',[2] or that a right is a liberty of a restricted kind, namely a liberty which is either protected, recognized, or at least allowed by the law.[3] The force of the equation makes itself felt both among those jurisprudents who allege that many so called 'rights', for example a right of way or of self-defence, the right of combination, the right to carry on a trade or business, are really only liberties,[4] and among those philosophers who, recognizing that, while one can have a right either to V or to be Ved, for example to give or be given, one can have a liberty only to V, for example to give, are, therefore, tempted to distinguish at least two different senses of 'right'.[5] Furthermore, though Hohfeld clearly and correctly wished to distinguish between a right and a liberty—or a privilege, as he usually called it—he wrongly argued, first, that these are two senses of 'right'—what his followers call a 'claim-right' and a 'liberty-right'—and, secondly, that the difference between either a right and a liberty or

---

[1] Hobbes, *Leviathan*, ch. 14; Spinoza, *Tractatus Theologico-Politicus*, ch. 16.

[2] e.g. Holmes (1881), 214; Kocourek (1927), 2; Dias (1970), 251 ff.; Raphael (1962), 348; Downie (1969), 116-26; Roshwald (1959); Becker (1977); Flathman (1976), 38 ff.; Wringe (1981), chs. 5 and 12.

[3] 'Protected', e.g. Lamont (1946), 71-8; Holmes (1881), 214; 'recognized', e.g. *Quinn* v. *Leathem* (1901) AC 534; 'allowed', e.g. Hobbes 'that liberty which the Civil Law leaves us', *Leviathan*, ch. 26.

[4] e.g. Williams (1956), 1132, 1136; Kocourek (1927), 2.

[5] e.g. Raphael (1962); Downie (1969). Mayo (1965), 224-5, seems to think that 'the right to V', as opposed to the right to be Ved, is only an idiom for 'it is right to V'.

a claim-right and a liberty-right is that the former of each pair implies, while the latter does not, a duty in someone else.

The plausibility of an equation of rights and liberties is strengthened by the fact that most of the famous Bills of Rights from Magna Carta to the United Nations Declaration of Human Rights mention and list, seemingly indifferently, both rights and liberties. Furthermore, the history of most struggles for human rights is largely an account of a fight for freedom against oppressive laws and governments.

Despite all this, an examination of the idea of *liberty* or *freedom* will show how different it is from that of *a right*.

(a) 'Free from' and 'free to'

The notion of freedom can be qualified in several ways whose variety is indicated, in English at least, by various grammatical devices. First, that whose freedom is at issue is that *of* which there is freedom or that which is *free*, whether it be freedom of thought, speech, movement, or the press, or a free man, will, choice, passage, house, or trade. In more general areas, this freedom can be characterized adjectively, for example as moral, political, religious, economic, personal, sexual, etc. freedom. Secondly, that whose absence makes free that which is free is that *from* which there is freedom or that *from* (or *of*) which it is free, whether it be freedom from superstition, poverty, blemish, or infection or being free from (or of) passion, temptation, noise, rust, or obstruction. Thirdly, that which is open to that which is free because of that absence which makes it free is that which it is free *to do*, whether a wheel is free to move, a plant to grow, an animal to roam, or a woman to marry. What it is free *to* is something in the area of that which it has freedom *of,* for example to have freedom of movement is to be free to move, of thought to think, of the will to will, of religion to practise one's religion, of conscience to consult and follow one's conscience. Those, such as intelligent creatures, who are capable of feeling something to be so can also *feel* free either from or to so and so, whether or not they actually are free.

It is because what something is 'free to do' indicates that which the absence of all it is free from allows it to engage in from its own nature and resources—no longer held back by that from which it is now free—that what someone or something is free to do encompasses only his or its action. Thus, a wheel can be free to move, but not to be moved, a plant to grow, but not to be grown, an animal to roam, but not to be taken for a walk, and a man to marry, but not to be married. Further, one can freely move, choose, surrender, sacrifice, etc., that is, do any of these without the presence of an extraneous factor. Similarly, nothing and nobody can be free to achieve or suffer so and so, to mean, deserve, need, be able to, equal, etc. such and such. Nor can anyone be free to feel any sensation or emotion, to want or expect, etc.

'Liberty' the Latinized form for what is expressed in Anglo-Saxon by 'freedom', seems to be used, nowadays at least, more restrictively, but not differently. Thus, so and so may have liberty or be at liberty and, hence, we can speak of liberty of conscience or speech, of the press or the people and, adjectively of political, religious, or personal liberty. So and so can have the liberty or be at liberty *to* do something, but not liberty *from* anything. The word 'liberty' is used normally only of animate creatures. A dog or a man, but not a thing, can, we say, be set at liberty, while only a person can have the liberty or be at liberty to V, whether it is to stop or to go, to accept or refuse. Hobbes, indeed, used 'liberty' of things, adding, quite rightly, that where 'freedom' and 'liberty' are used of both the animate and the inanimate, they are used in the same sense.[6] And modern writers on morals and politics often explicitly use 'liberty' and 'freedom' interchangeably.[7]

Because sometimes what interests us is what so and so is

---

[6] *Leviathan*, ch. 21.
[7] e.g. Berlin (1958), 6; Knight (1962), 110; Gewirth (1982), ch. 13; Crocker (1980); as also did Locke, *2nd Treatise, passim*.

free *from*, whether it be disease, traffic, persecution, or temptation, it is left open or unclear what, if anything, this makes it free *to* do, and, contrariwise, when what interests us is what it is free *to* do, for example to grow, to run, or to marry, it is left open or unclear *from* what it is free. What is a sky free from clouds free to do or a bridge free to expand free from? Is a person free from persecution free to marry rather than to study or a person free to move free from bonds rather than from rules? To ask how free someone is may be to ask *from* how much he is free or how much he is free *to* do, though the two enquiries may be contingently connected. One group may fight for freedom from the imposition of a certain brand of religion, while another fights for the freedom to impose that brand. It may be, indeed, that freedom *from* is more basic than freedom *to* in that whatever is free to do so and so is also free from such and such but not vice versa. What is free to move, grow, run, or expand is free from some particular impediment which would constrain it from doing these, whereas what is free from disease, traffic, persecution, fault, or temptation is not thereby free to do anything specific. It is not necessary that everything which is free should both be free from something and free to do something.[8] Nor is it true that what is free to V must be equally free not to V. My duty to V allows me freedom to V but not freedom not to V, just as the necessity of Ving allows the possibility of Ving but not of not Ving.

Both the freedom of, the freedom from, and the freedom to such and such have degrees. So and so can be partly or completely free from disease or free to grow; both its freedom from interference and its freedom to move can be increased or limited, enlarged or restricted. This is all equally true of freedom of movement or of the press. Whether logically a certain freedom can be exercised, fought for, pursued, protected, relinquished, violated, or restrained depends not on the notion of freedom, but on whose freedom

[8] *Pace* MacCallum (1967).

it is and what it is a freedom from or to. Inanimate objects don't exercise, fight for, or relinquish their freedom; nor could one violate, deprive, pursue, or restrain a freedom from temptation, infection, or rust or a freedom to expand. Yet such objects are, nevertheless, free to do some things and free from others. There is no good reason to suppose that 'free' is used differently of people and of things or of the social and the political.

None of these distinctions within the notion of freedom gives any reason for alleging or introducing two (or more) concepts of freedom or senses of 'free'.[9] Certainly, one can in some cases be more interested in what someone or something is or should be free from, whether it is noise or disease, persecution or poverty, and in other cases in what someone or something is or should be free to do, whether it is to expand or unwind, to live in peace or to vote, and no doubt at various periods in political thought freedom *from* so and so—what has sometimes been called 'negative freedom'—and freedom *to* do such and such—what has sometimes been called 'positive freedom'—have each occupied the stage. But 'freedom from' and 'freedom to' no more express two concepts of *freedom* than, for example, 'flying from' and 'flying to' or 'safe from' and 'safe to' express two concepts of *flying* or *safety*. It is as mistaken to think of 'freedom from' and 'freedom to' as two different concepts as to contrast a right to protection from and a right to provision of as different concepts,[10] though, of course, at different times in history emphasis has been laid more on what one wishes to escape from than on what one wishes to enter into.

An important consequence of distinguishing 'freedom from' and 'freedom to' as two different concepts, one negative and one positive, is that the need is then felt to add to the negative characterization of 'freedom from', in terms of

[9] As does Berlin (1958); cp. Jones (1962); Howe (1962). Contrast Mac-Callum (1967), who nevertheless thinks 'free' is used differently of persons and things.
[10] Kamenka (1978), 5.

the *absence* of something, a positive characterization of 'freedom to' in terms of a *source*, cause, or explanation of what one is free to do. Almost invariably this positive source is identified as a possibility, ability, or power in that which is free to V. An old legal maxim, for instance, says 'Libertas est *potestas* faciendi id quod iure licet', while Locke, and Cicero before him, defines 'liberty' as 'the *power* a man has to do or forbear doing any particular action . . . as he himself wills it'.[11]

The history of philosophy, indeed, includes those, such as Hobbes,[12] Bentham, Mill, Russell, Sidgwick, Schlick, and Marx, who analyse freedom (or liberty) negatively as the absence of something, those, such as Aristotle, Descartes, Locke, and Leibniz, who analyse it positively as a certain power and those, such as Hume,[13] Edwards, Priestley, Montesquieu, and Green, who include both a negative and a positive aspect in their analyses. Similarly, analyses of freedom of the will range over a spectrum from the negative characteristic of absence of control by others or by parts of oneself, such as one's desires, inclinations, etc., to the positive characteristic of being autonomous, self-controlled, or with the power of choice. The assumption of a positive element in freedom is well illustrated by the current fashion, dating back at least to G. E. Moore's *Ethics* of 1910—though as old as Locke—of equating the problem of free will with the question whether 'we have the power of acting differently from the way in which we actually do act' or whether 'we *can* do what we don't do'. So a recent article, Davidson's 'Freedom to Act' in 1973, equated 'free to do' and 'can do'

[11] Locke, *Essay, II. xxi.* 15; cp. 8, 14, 27; though contrast his negative definition in, e.g. *2nd Treatise*, s. 57, 'liberty is freedom from restraint and violence from others'; Cicero, *Paradoxa Stoicorum*, v. 34.

[12] *Leviathan* chs. 14, 21; though he added that the impediments whose absence was freedom are impediments 'which take away one's power'.

[13] *Enquiry* VIII.I; cp. Gewirth (1982), ch. 13. Crocker's (1980) contrast of 'positive' and 'negative' freedom is really a contrast of more and fewer constraints on negative freedom, though he sometimes takes positive freedom to be the presence of alternatives. And he is explicitly more interested in a persuasive than a descriptive definition of 'liberty'.

and concluded that 'freedom to act is a causal power of the agent'.

Freedom (or liberty) and power (or ability), however, are quite different and unrelated concepts; being free (or at liberty) to V neither implies, nor is implied by, having the power or ability to V. Somebody or something can have a power or ability, for example to move, at those moments when it or he is not free to exercise that power or ability. To lack freedom of movement or of speech is not to lack the ability to move or to speak, but to have some constraint on exercising any such ability. There are, indeed, many things which people and material objects have the ability or power to do, which it does not even make sense to say they are free to do. Some flowers are able to withstand certain degrees of frost, but this is not something they are free to do; some people have the ability to see further than others, but they do not have a freedom which others lack. The obstacle or difficulty which prevents me from reaching, seeing, discovering, or in some way attaining so and so makes me unable to do this, but does not make me not free to do it. In general, one can have the power or ability both to attempt things and to bring them off, but be free only to attempt them. Contrariwise, though what so and so is free to do it always makes sense to say it is able to do, somebody or something can in fact be free to do what it or he has, for some reason, no power or ability to do. I may be perfectly free to suggest a better alternative, but be unable to do so. To give a plant freedom to spread by clearing the space around it is not to give it the ability to spread. Further, to say that someone is free to think, assume, or suspect what he likes is not to talk of his ability or power to do these. Nor would one who lacked some physical or mental ability, for example to ride a bicycle or to speak French, be properly described as not being free to do these. Indeed, even if lack of ability could be a reason for one's lack of freedom—as those contend who suggest that a deaf man is not free to hear—the former cannot be the same as the latter.

What gives or takes away, increases or decreases, so and so's freedom does not necessarily give or take away, increase or decrease, its ability; or vice versa. Freedom is increased or decreased by taking away or adding some constraint, ability is increased or decreased in itself. To give so and so the freedom to V is usually to remove a constraint to the exercise of any ability (or power) it has, to enable it to exercise those abilities (or powers), not to give it an extra ability (or power) it did not possess before. An explanation of somebody's or something's powers is not the same as an explanation of why or how they are free to do so and so or such and such.

If the supposition of a positive element in freedom, such as an ability or power, is, as I have argued, a mistake,[14] what about the negative element? The root idea in freedom, I suggest, is that of *absence*, whether that which is absent is specifically mentioned as that which so and so is free from or whether mention is only made of that which is now, because of this absence, open to so and so to do or whether what is mentioned is only the area in regard to which the absence of the unmentioned item leaves open what is also unmentioned.

But not all absence is freedom. A man without a wife, a number without a factor, a country without a king, a course without any participants, etc. would not normally be said to be free from what it is without. The absence must be of something which was impinging on or affecting or would ·impinge on or affect in some way that which is made free by its absence. Attempts, however, to make this notion of impinging or affecting more specific usually fail because they depend too much on the narrow set of examples chosen. Thus, 'interference' is too narrow an idea to explain, for example, 'free meal' or 'freelance', or even human freedom from temptation or disease; 'being bound' is too narrow to

[14] Cp. Whateley, *Logic* (1869), 137: ' "Liberty", which is a purely negative term, denoting merely "absence of restraint", is sometimes confounded with "Power".'

explain any of these or 'free from noise or rust'; 'restraint' (or 'constraint'), the idea used by Mill and many others, is too narrow to explain 'free from traffic', 'free from fault'. Nor is there anything in the idea that what someone is free to do is necessarily something he wants to do.[15] Circumstances can leave me as free to dismiss an employee as to retain him, whichever I want. Further, though someone who is coerced is to that extent not free, he who is not free from blame or free to marry is not necessarily coerced. Even if lack of political freedom is linked with human interference,[16] this is a consequence of its being political, not of its being lack of freedom. It is also too extreme to hold that what something is free from is necessarily a defect or that what he or it is free to do is a merit. An area can be free from traffic, an institution free from regulations, and a youth free from parental control whatever the value of these. To be free to murder or to rebel does not imply that these are good things. Nor—what is a different point—need freedom from X or freedom to V be itself necessarily a good thing. Freedom from doubt about the rightness of one's actions or freedom to steal are not meritorious.

The analytic question of what it means to say that something, whether a person, a state, or anything else, is free must not be confused with the evaluative question about what it must be free from or free to do in order to be honoured as a free state or a free person.[17] The evaluative question asks us to decide between the various things from which or to do which the state or person is free. Is a citizen free because what he is free from are political, economic, religious, or legal bonds, because he is free to V or free to F? Furthermore, to say that someone or something is free is elliptical, since he or it can be free from, or free to do, one thing while not free from, or to do, another. I may be free because I am free from university commitments or free to attend to you,

---

[15] *Pace* Berlin (1958), 7; Mill, *On Liberty*, ch. V; cp. Hobbes, 'not hindered to do what he hath the will to do'.

[16] As Berlin (1958), 7, contends.

[17] e.g. Milne (1968), ch. 5; Crocker (1980), *passim*.

while not free from worry or free to go on holiday. A bathroom is usually free because it is free from occupants, but not necessarily free from dirt or from a destruction order.

(b) *Liberties and rights*

Having examined the notion of freedom (or liberty), we can see that rights are quite different from freedoms.[18] First of all, there can only be a right *to* something, whereas freedom can be either freedom *to* so and so or freedom *from* such and such. While both persons and things can be free,[19] either *to* or *from*, it is, as I have shown earlier, at the very least debatable whether things can have rights. Moreover, a person can be physically as well as legally, morally, or regulatively free, but there is no such thing as a physical right. Various freedoms occur in charters of human rights, but one does not talk of human or natural liberties in the way one does of human or natural rights. There are degrees of freedom, but not of rights. I can be more or less free, but not more or less have a right. Though both a right and a liberty (or freedom) can be had or given, claimed, demanded, or fought for, recognized or protected, relinquished or forfeited, violated or abridged; liberties (or freedom), unlike rights, cannot be delegated or transferred, usurped or waived. Furthermore, 'free' is something which, for example, a plant or a wheel can be, although it makes no sense to talk of its exercising, pursuing, or relinquishing its freedom. 'A right', by contrast, is not, I argued earlier, something a subject could have if it makes no sense to talk of such a subject, or type of subject, exercising, claiming or forfeiting its rights. Though both what we can sensibly have a right to do and what we can be free to do exclude many things—so that we cannot either have a right to, or be free to, achieve or suffer anything, to deserve, dislike, dread, or regret anything, to dream, imagine, intend, or mean, to need or want, etc.—what we can have a right to, unlike what we can be

[18] Cp. Austin (1861).
[19] Though, perhaps, things cannot have a liberty.

free to, includes having something done to us. We can have a right, but not be free, to be consulted or protected, to be given help, information, or security and thus have a right, but not a liberty, to special consideration, a living wage, education, etc. Nor should the difference between the sensible notion of having a right to be Ved and the nonsense of being free to be Ved be explained away by the gratuitous introduction of two senses of 'right'.[20] It is the difference between 'having a right' and 'being free' which explains why some of the things we can have a right to, including not only to have something done to us, such as to be protected, but also to feel something, such as to feel annoyed at our treatment, or to know something, such as what we are accused of, are not things we can sensibly be said to be free to.

We have seen that in modern usage, though not in that of Hobbes and Locke, the Latin form 'liberty' is more restricted than the Anglo-Saxon 'freedom'. We don't, for instance, nowadays talk of a liberty from, of the liberty of inanimate objects, or of physical liberties. In other respects, however, liberties differ from rights exactly as freedoms do.

Even when what we have a right to do and what we are free or at liberty to do are the same, being free or at liberty to V does not imply having a right to V. Thus, even the most callow student is free to criticize a great scholar, but the right to criticize, we feel, has to be earned by those who have faced up to the difficulties themselves. Though many people may be at liberty to ask favours of me, only those attached to me in various ways have the right to do so. Freedom of entry may be allowed to all tourists, but only natives may have a right to entry. Nor does what leaves one free to V, as when refraining from committing oneself to a certain course leaves one free to take an alternative, necessarily give one a right to pursue the alternative. The right to be free is a precious thing, whereas the freedom to be free is a piece

[20] e.g. Raphael (1962), 348; Downie (1969), 116; Kocourek (1927), 2; or by the confinement of a right to what we can have done to us, e.g. Williams (1956), 1145.

of nonsense. A right is often introduced to guard, legally or morally, the corresponding freedom, but a liberty cannot intelligibly be introduced to guard the corresponding right. Conversely, one may not be free to exercise one's right, but one cannot lack the right to exercise it. To say that someone has a right to V may be either to report a fact or to make an evaluation, to describe or prescribe, whereas to say that he is free to V can only be to report a fact or, at most, to grant permission. Having the right to V provides a justification for Ving, whereas being free to V provides only a source or condition for Ving. We can ask 'by what right', but not 'by what liberty', someone does something. Hence, the law must provide explicitly for one's legal rights, but need not, though it can, for one's legal liberties. One is at liberty, but does not necessarily have a right, to do anything which is not explicitly excluded. To be excused, exempted, relieved, released, or made immune from something is, to that extent, to be given some freedom; but not necessarily to be given any right. Whereas one can give freedom only to one who has already been restricted, namely by removing his restrictions, even the already free can be given a right as something additional.

Modern jurists usually recognize that there is an important difference between a right and a liberty, either by holding, correctly, that the two concepts are quite different or by holding, incorrectly, that, though there is a sense of 'right' in which it is the same as a liberty, there is also a sense, perhaps the strict sense, in which it is not the same. Furthermore, they usually admit that this difference is that liberty (or freedom) is a negative concept, while right is a positive concept. That *liberty* (or freedom) is a negative concept was stressed even by those who equated it with *right*.[21] In the law liberty implies an absence of any duty, in morals an absence of any obligation, to do otherwise.[22] It is, indeed, this negative

[21] Hobbes, *Leviathan*, ch. 14, 'the absence of external impediment'.
[22] For the law, see Hohfeld (1919); Pound (1959), IV. ch. 23; Williams (1956); Dias (1970).

feature of freedom which has misled some jurisprudents to suppose that freedom is a non-legal concept on the ground that it is something outside the law.[23] But just as being physically free means being without any physical impingement, so being legally free—as when I am legally free to marry because I have no living spouse—means being without any legal impingement.

Right, on the other hand, is a positive concept. The mere absence of an obligation or duty allows, but does not entitle, one to do anything. It is far too liberal to suppose that everything that we are not expressly forbidden, whether legally or morally, to do, we have a right to do.[24] This is why the thesis, advocated by Bentham and some moderns, that having a right to V is merely having no duty, or obligation, not to V is mistaken.[25] Hence, to ask what gives someone the right to V is not merely to ask what leaves him free to V. Freedom suggests a *de facto* absence of something, such as an interference; a right a *de iure* absence. We can talk of rights, but not of freedom or liberties, which we have in virtue of our nature. The air of paradox about the statement that someone did so and so, though he was not free to do it, vanishes from the statement that he did it, though he had no right to do it.

But what is this positive aspect of a right by which it is distinguished from a mere liberty or freedom?

It cannot be just the fact that a corresponding freedom to V is recognized or protected, for example by the law.[26] For, in the first place, rights can as easily as liberties be either protected and recognized or unprotected and unrecognized; and, in the second, a right may, as we saw, have no corresponding freedom, as when one has a right to be treated in a certain way. Nor can it be, as philosophers and jurisprudents commonly suggest, that a right to V is a freedom to

[23] e.g. Kocourek (1930), 250-2.
[24] McCloskey (1965), 116.
[25] e.g. Bowring III. 181, 217-18; (1789), ch. XVI. 26; Raphael (1967), 54-67; Dworkin (1977a), 189; Wringe (1981), 46.
[26] e.g. Hobbes, Holmes, Lamont.

V with the addition of an obligation or a duty on others not to interfere.[27] For, first, as I have just mentioned, many rights, such as to be treated in various ways, have no corresponding freedoms. Secondly, as I argued at length earlier, many rights have no correlative duties. It is significant that attempts to meet this latter objection have led some to hold that many of the instances which are ordinarily called 'rights', both within and without the law, for which there are admittedly no correlative duties, are not rights at all, but only liberties.[28] Examples are the 'right' of entry, of self-defence, of free speech, of combination, of way, the 'right' to carry on a trade or profession, to build on the edge of one's land, or to practise as a medical practitioner. A famous set of instances comprises the cases of trade competition and union disputes, discussed earlier, which led Hohfeld and his followers to allege that the courts had confused rights with liberties or privileges. The *reductio ad absurdum* of these attempts is the thesis that there is no such thing as a right to act.[29] There is, it is said, only a liberty to act and a right that others should or should not act on one.

A right is not any kind of liberty, or freedom.[30] For not only is a right, as I have earlier argued, of quite a different kind from a freedom (or liberty), it does not even necessarily imply it. Clearly one can have a right, moral or legal, which one is not circumstantially free to exercise. But, more importantly, though one has such a right, one may not even be morally free to exercise it because one may have opposing moral obligations. Thus, I may have a right, by virtue of my position, to do so and so, but be not free, because of a promise or some other moral constraint, to do it. I shall argue later that the positive nature of a right, as contrasted

[27] e.g. Haworth (1968), 64; (1977/8), 95; cp. Williams (1956), 1136 ff.; Stell (1979), 10–11; McCloskey (1979).

[28] e.g. Williams (1956).

[29] e.g. Kocourek (1927); cp. Williams (1956), 1145.

[30] *Pace* Flathman (1976), ch. 7, who slips from 'having a right' to 'exercising a right'.

with the negative nature of freedom or liberty, consists in
an antecedent characteristic, namely the presence of a title
in the holder of the right, by which he is entitled to what he
has a right to.

10

Powers

The equation of the notions of *right* and *power* goes back at least to William of Ockham, one of the first philosophers to offer an analysis of rights.[1] Spinoza and, sometimes, Hobbes regarded rights as powers,[2] though, perhaps, Spinoza does not always make it clear whether he regards the two as equivalent or whether, as seems more common, he is only stressing that any individual's right, whether of a person or the state, is coextensive with and determined by its power.[3] Although Locke insisted that a wrongly acquired power over something did not give a right to it,[4] he frequently speaks indifferently of a power over so and so and a right or title to it.[5] Indeed, his thesis that a conquerer's power over the life of the defeated does not give him a right or title to the latter's possessions is also expressed as the thesis that a right in regard to the life does not give a right in regard to the possessions.[6] These philosophers have been followed by many jurisprudents.[7] Some, such as Bentham, Salmond, and Terry, explicitly classed powers as one kind of rights.[8] And even those who clearly distinguish the two often differ both between themselves and within their own writings as to whether so and so, for example the sale of goods, a wife's

[1] *Opus Nonaginta Dierum*, ch. 65; cp. Villey (1962), 240-1.

[2] Spinoza, *Tractatus Politicus* II. 4, III. 2; cp. T. H. Green, *Political Obligation* (1966), 40-1; Hobbes, *De Cive* I. 14.

[3] *Tractatus Theologico-Politicus*, ch. XVI and *Tractatus Politicus*, chs. II and III.

[4] *2nd Treatise*, ss. 196, 199.

[5] ss. 3, 67, ch. XVI.

[6] ss. 180, 182.

[7] Cp. Olivecrona (1939), 89 and ch. 3 *passim*, and references in Pound (1959), IV. 68 n 59.

[8] Bentham (1970), 84, 139, 220. In (1789), ch. XVI, 25, n. 1, he says power is not a species of right, but to have a power implies to have a right to the power. Salmond (1902), s. 76; T. H. Terry, *Leading Principles of Anglo-American Law* (1884), ss. 113-17. Contrast Bierling, quoted Pound (1959), IV. 94.

pledging of her husband's credit, a landowner's removal of a trespasser, is a right or a power.[9] Hohfeld alleges that often when the courts use 'rights' they ought to be using 'powers'.[10]

Several reasons may be suggested for this assimilation of powers and rights. First, many of the sorts of things one can have the power to do are things one can have the right to do, and vice versa, for example to appoint, to arrest, to destroy, to sell, to pledge, to suspend, to requisition, etc.; and many of the areas, such as the legal, political, or judicial, where one operates are areas where the other does also. Secondly, there is the jurists' tendency to emphasize, as the core of the notion of power, the idea of altering an existing legal condition or position.[11] Such an emphasis overlooks the way in which the exercise of a right to V may have the same consequences as the exercise of a power to V. Thirdly, the idea of power was often extended to right because of the thesis that a right is essentially the power to demand or claim the performance of a duty in another. This was why Pound classed both rights and powers as 'conceptions of control'.[12] Fourthly, the equation of rights and powers may be due to the twin assumptions that rights are the same as (or a sub-class of) liberties and that liberties, at least in their positive aspect, are powers or abilities; from which it could be concluded that rights are powers. We have, however, seen that both of these twin assumptions are mistaken; hence their conclusion is not proved.

The notions of a *power* and a *right* are actually quite different both within and without the law. First, in its widest context a power can belong either to a person or a thing, for example the power to move or to change so and

[9] J. Stone (1946) calls pledging of husband's credit a right on p. 118 and a power on p. 123; Dias (1970) calls it a power. Dias says the so called 'right' to sell goods is a 'power'.

[10] e.g. (1919), 51 ff. and 54, n. 73; cp. Washington Law and contrast Scott J. in Hohfeld, 51, n. 65.

[11] e.g. Hohfeld (1919), 50 ff.; Pound (1959); Dias (1970).

[12] (1959), IV. 114 etc.

o, whereas only a person—and perhaps an animal—can
have a right. Secondly, what a person can have a right to
do is sometimes logically different from what he can have
a power to do. One can have either a power or a right to act,
but only a right to be acted on. One can, for example, have
the right, but not the power, to be fed and clothed, to be
treated as an equal, to be represented in Parliament, or to
education, an adequate standard of living. One can also have
the right, but not the power, for example, to feel hard done
by, to be indignant, etc. On the other hand, one can have
the power either to do or achieve but only the right to do.
The usual jurisprudential definition of a power as an ability
or capacity to alter an existing position has the merit of
emphasizing that a power is a power to bring about something, whether the bringing about is an action or an achievement.[13] Powers have effects, whereas rights have only
consequences. To have a power is to have control. Where
the idea of control is absent, as over what is done to one
or what one feels, so is the idea of power, but not that of
right. One has powers over, but rights at most against, so
and so. One can get someone into or make them subject to
one's power, but not into or subject to one's rights.

Even where it makes sense both to have a power to V and
a right to V, having one neither implies nor is implied by
the other. The university regulations may give a student the
right to take either a subsidiary or two ancillaries; they do
not give him a power to make this choice. Conversely, the
power which the regulations give Senate to appoint examiners
is not the right to do so. To give a minority group the right
to speak their own language is not to give them a power,
nor is to give an official the power to grant pensions to give
him a right to do this. Police powers are not police rights.
Someone auctioning goods which unknown to him are stolen
has the power to alienate them, but, because of a duty not
to, has no right to do so.[14] In the cases, *Pryce* v. *Belcher*

[13] Cp. Dias (1970); Kocourek (1927); Cp. Pound (1959), ch. 22 'capacity of
creating, directing or altering'.   [14] Cp. Tapper (1973), 272.

ruled that the power to compel a returning officer to put one's name on the poll was not a right to compel him.[15] Lord Esher in *Attorney-General* v. *Sudeley* said 'what is called "a right of action" is not the power of bringing an action. Anybody can bring an action though he has no right at all'.[16] To admit that I do not have the power to grant this or to stop that is to proclaim my ineffectiveness; to say I do not have the right is to express my lack of justification.

On the other hand, one cannot show that powers and rights are mutually non-implicative by the common philosopher's practice of instancing, for example, a legal right which one is physically powerless to exercise or a physical power which one has no legal right to exercise,[17] for an analogous argument would fallaciously show that a power is not a power at all by instancing legal powers without corresponding physical powers and physical powers which one has no legal power to exercise. To show that powers and rights are different and independent, one must, as one can, exemplify both from the same field.

Thirdly, powers, but not rights, can be physical as well as non-physical. Though there are legal, statutory, and executive rights as well as powers, there are no physical or psychological rights. One can have both the physical and the legal power to remove a trespasser, but only the legal right to do so. Fourthly, though both rights and (non-physical) powers can be given to one person by another, only powers can be delegated or transferred. Although one can give another both the same rights and the same powers as one's self, one can pass on to another one's powers, but not one's own rights.

Fifthly, the notion of *power* goes with those of ability and of authority;[18] while the notion of *right* goes with those of entitlement and justification. To ask what gives you the power to V is to ask what enables or authorizes you to V; to ask what gives you the right to V is to ask what entitles

[15] (1847) 4 CB 866; *Niblett* v. *Confectionery Materials Co.* [1921] 3 KB 387.
[16] [1869] I QB 354 at 359.
[17] e.g.Hart (1974), 43; McCloskey (1965), 115; Benn and Peters (1959), 91.
[18] Cp. *Remington* v. *Parkins* (1873) 10 RI 550, 553 (quoted Hohfeld 51).

you to V. Being given the length of X may enable, but cannot sensibly entitle, you to discover or calculate the length of Y, but it may both enable and entitle you to conclude or infer that Y is such and such a length. Being a friend of the family can give me the right, but not the power, to be consulted on such and such an occasion; whereas being the family solicitor can give me the power, but not the right, to draw up the head of the family's will. Rights, but not powers, can be infringed or violated; while powers, but not rights, can be controlled or restrained. Unlike rights, powers can be great or feeble, failing or increasing, effective or ineffective. Rights need a justification, whereas powers can be arbitrary. The difference between having the power to V and having the right to V or between being enabled to V and being entitled to V is akin to that between having reasons which lead one to think that p and having reasons which justify one in thinking that p.

Sixthly, it is authorities or those to whom authority has been given who typically have non-physical powers; whereas it is subjects who typically have rights. A power is a bit of control over others, while a right is often a bit of freedom from the control of others. Sovereigns seek powers, while slaves seek rights. There is a sort of hierarchy with powers at the top and rights at the bottom. Between the top and the bottom of the hierarchy are those with powers over those below them and with rights against those above them. This is why it is often perfectly sensible for the same thing to be either a power or a right, for example to pledge one's husband's credit, to requisition a ship, to fine on the spot, etc. In law the cases make it perfectly clear that many of these things are considered both as rights and powers.[19] This is also why one cannot have a right—as one can have a power—to achieve, since this would entail controlling something else; nor, on the other hand, can one have a power—

---

[19] Hohfeld (1919), 51, n. 65, *Mabre* v. *Whittaker* (1906) where the law says 'right' and the judge says 'power'; and Hohfeld, p. 53, n. 71, *Emery* v. *Clough* (1885) 'right or power of defeasance'.

as one can have a right—to be treated in a certain way, since this would entail being controlled by someone else. Because power is linked with bringing about something, legal powers are commonly those of creating, diverting, or altering the existing scene.

The different positions of authority in morals and in politics explain why powers, unlike rights, play almost no part in the former and a dominant part in the latter.

11

Privileges

Another notion that has commonly been either confused with, assimilated to or equated with *a right* is that of *privilege*. Even those who have properly distinguished the two have often done so on the wrong grounds and in the wrong way. It will help to throw light on the nature of a right to see its exact relations to that of a privilege.

(a) *Privilege*

Many jurisprudents have assumed that *privilege* is a notion co-ordinate with *right, duty, liberty, power, immunity*, etc., and have, therefore, placed it in the same table as these others. They have differed simply on the position of such a place; some supposing a privilege to be a right, others a power and others a liberty. I shall argue that *privilege* does not share the same *fundamentum divisionis* as these other notions; that it is, in fact, of a different logical order. Any one of the things covered by these other notions can be, but need not be, a privilege. What makes anything a privilege is a particular characteristic of the circumstances in which it occurs. It is as mistaken to attempt to place the notion of privilege amongst these other notions as it would be to attempt, for example, to co-ordinate the notion of a *gift* with such notions as *car, house*, or *boat*, etc., though any one of the things covered by these notions can be, but need not be, a gift. *Privilege* is neither the correlative nor the opposite of *right* or *duty*, any more than *gift* is the correlative or opposite of *house* or *boat*. Nor is the word 'privilege' ambiguous, with a different sense corresponding to each of these other words, any more than the word 'gift' is ambiguous, with as many meanings as there are kinds of gifts.

Furthermore, I shall try to show that the legal notion of *privilege* is the same as that expressed by the word 'privilege' in its everyday use.

'Privilegium' indicated in Roman times one example of a kind of law aimed specifically at single persons or cases, whether by conferring an advantage, such as a right, which would be a 'favourable' privilege, or a disadvantage, such as a duty, which would be an 'odious' privilege. For example, an act granting an inventor exclusive selling rights in his invention would be a 'favourable' privilege and an Act of Attainder an 'odious' privilege. 'Privilege' in its modern legal use differs, as Austin pointed out, in that it applies to what is conferred by the law rather than to the law which confers it, and is confined solely to favourable privileges.[1] Thus, persons who cannot be sued, such as foreign diplomats, but not persons who cannot sue, such as enemy aliens, are said to be privileged.

'Privilege', both in its legal and its everday use, indicates that someone or something has been singled out for advantageous treatment. A privilege is necessarily reserved for a sub-set, not given to all; whether the sub-set are individuals, groups or occasions. There can be a privileged few, but not a privileged many. There are privileged persons, places, and classes, privileged offices, occasions, documents, and circumstances. Many people have supposed that psychologically each of us has a privileged access to his own thoughts. It is this essential characteristic of preferential treatment which explains why privileges often fail to get the good press usually enjoyed by rights.

Privileges can be granted or taken away, held, enjoyed, won, or lost. A privilege can be positive, that is, allow someone to do something which others cannot do or which he in other circumstances cannot do, or negative, that is, free him from restrictions under which others, or he in other circumstances, labour. Many privileges are given individually, while others are given to a class in virtue of its position or

[1] (1861), Lecture 28.

circumstances. There are various reasons, logical, moral, and historical, why particular classes or circumstances happen to be privileged.[2] A privilege can take the form of a particular act or happening or experience, as when I once had the privilege of being entertained by a family of the French provincial aristocracy or of working with Einstein; or it can take the form of a type of action or happening, as when one has the privilege of wearing one's hat in the presence of the Queen. It can also take the form of a power, liberty, immunity, chance, opportunity, or right, as when a particular body has as a privilege the power to grant licences, the legislature has the power to compel the attendance of witnesses, or when someone has the liberty to wear one's hat in the presence of the Queen, has an immunity from parking fines, a chance or opportunity to hear Callas sing in a private house, or a right to present a bill in Parliament. Parliamentary and court proceedings are privileged in that, unlike the general run of speech-making occasions, they give rise to no action for defamation.[3] The privileges of office may include all sorts of things. To take away a person's privileges is to take away any of the things, whether rights, powers, liberties, exemptions, immunities, which he was given as a privilege.

But though any one of these can be a privilege, there is no one of these forms which a privilege necessarily takes. The privilege of wearing one's hat in the presence of the Queen is not a power, but a liberty;[4] the privilege of granting licences to applicants is not a liberty, but a power; the privilege of not paying a parking fee is a, perhaps diplomatic, immunity, not a power or liberty; the privilege of hearing

[2] Cp. Pound (1959), IV. 131–43.

[3] e.g. James (1969), ch. 13, s. 7; cf. *Re Parliamentary Privilege Act* [1958] 2 All ER 329; *Szalatnay* v. *Fink* [1956] 1 All ER 717. On court proceedings, cf. *More* v. *Weaver* [1928] 2 KB 520.

[4] Cf. *Goldsack* v. *Shore* [1950] 1 KB 708, 714 *per* Evershed MR: 'If the nature of the privilege given is a mere licence . . .'; *Matthews* v. *People* 202 Ill. 389, 401 (1903) *per* Magruder CJ: 'It is now well settled that the privilege of contracting is both a liberty and a property right' (quoted Hohfeld p. 49, n. 64); *Clifford* v. *O'Neill* 12 App. Div. 17; 42 NY Sup. 607, 609 (1896).

Callas sing is none of these. A gratuitous grant of a privileged licence to enter one's land or house is not the grant of a right.[5] Most importantly, though a particular right can be a privilege, and a privilege can take the form of a right, it is simply a mistake to suggest, as dictionaries—and, we shall see, jurisprudents and judges—sometimes do, that the meaning of 'right' is privilege or that a privilege is a species of right. That this is a mistake is clear not only from the fact that other things than rights can be privileges, but from the fact that not all rights are privileges. A particular right—or a particular power, liberty, or immunity—could be held by everyone, but it would be a contradiction to speak of a universal privilege.[6] In defamation, a plea of privilege is open only in particular cases, whereas a plea of justification is open in all.[7] A witness's right to silence is a privilege granted to certain witnesses in certain circumstances, for example in regard to solicitor–client communications.

To have or be given a privilege is to have or be given something as a privilege in the same way that to have or be given a gift is to have or be given something as a gift. And just as many different kinds of things, such as objects, skills, powers, position, etc., can be gifts, though a gift as such is not any of these, that is, is neither an object, a skill, a power or a position, so a privilege as such is not any of the many things, such as a right, a power, an immunity, an experience, which can be privileges. What makes anything a gift is its being something which has been given for nothing and what makes anything a privilege is its being something advantageous which is bestowed on only a few, whether it be a person, occasion, or office, etc. It is something preferential. Hence, it is equally mistaken either to single out any one of these,

[5] *Thomas* v. *Sorell* (1673), Vaughan 331, 351; Lurton J. in *City of Owensboro* v. *Cumberland Telephones, etc. Co.* 230 US 58, 64; 33 Sup. Ct. 988, 990 (1913) (quoted Hohfeld, n. 61a).

[6] Contrast J. Stone (1968), 144, n. 22, who appears to misunderstand the objections of Pound and Paton. Hawkins J. in *Allen* v. *Flood* [1898] AC 1. at 18 does say of a particular type of action that 'every person has a privilege . . .'.

[7] Cf. Williams (1956), 1132; *More* v. *Weaver* [1928] 2 KB 520; *Minter* v. *Priest* [1930] AC 558.

for example right or power, as explaining the nature of privilege or to suppose that, since any one of them can be a privilege, the word 'privilege' has different senses, for example that of 'right', 'power', etc.[8] And it is mistaken in the same way as it would be to suppose either that a gift is one of its species, such as car, or that the word 'gift' has as many meanings as there are kinds of gifts.

To suggest, for example, that a privilege is a right or that a right is a privilege, that is, that to be a privilege is to be a right—as contrasted with admitting that particular rights can be privileges and particular privileges can be rights— is to be misled by the verb 'to be' into assimilating two quite different concepts. It is analogous to the mistake of supposing that a gift as such is a boat or a boat is a gift; that is, to be a gift is to be a boat, just because a gift can on occasions be a boat and a boat can on occasion be a gift.

Anything, including rights, powers, liberties, etc., can be, but nothing need be, a privilege. It is a privilege if its conferment or possession sets one above others. Jurisprudents, from Austin onwards and including Hohfeld, usually admit, and sometimes emphasize, that the idea of a special advantage to a select individual or group is central to both the ordinary and the legal concept of a privilege.[9] Furthermore, Hohfeld sees that—'not infrequently' as he says—the idea of privilege may be applied to anything, whether a right, power, or immunity, to which the idea of special advantage applies. So also Kocourek, whose own thesis is that a privilege is a form of power exemplified by an exemption from duty, rather grudgingly admits that 'the tendency in professional speech is to confine the term privilege to forms of power

---

[8] Kocourek (1927), e.g., commits both of these fallacies; e.g. pp. 24, 83, 125–8 for the former and pp. 8–9, notes 2 and 3 for the latter.

[9] Austin (1861); Hohfeld (1919), 44–5; Bower (1932), 315; Williams (1956); Pound (1959), IV. 81, 114; Paton (1974), 292; Miller (1903), 103–8; 5 Viner, Abridgement (1965), s.v. 'Privilege'; cp. *Humphrey* v. *Pegues* (1872) 16 Wall 244, 247, *per* Hunt J. quoted in Hohfeld, p. 45, 'a peculiar benefit or advantage, a special exemption from a burden falling on others'; cf. Luxmoore LJ in *Le Strange* v. *Pettefar* (1939) 161 LTR 300 ' "privilege" describes . . . a right enjoyed by a few as opposed to a right enjoyed by all'.

which confer a special advantage on the dominus not enjoyed in general; in other words, exemption from duty is the normal situation'.[10] In fact, there runs through Kocourek's account of privilege, especially in the more detailed treatment of the notion in his *Jural Relations*, an ambivalence between the view that a privilege is merely a reciprocal of power, that is, that whereas power is a capability of doing something positive, privilege is a capability of declining a negative act, and the view that privilege is 'a capability which departs from the general rule' or even simply 'an abnormal situation differing from the general rule'.[11]

(b) *Privileges, rights, and liberties*

Many jurisprudents, however, identify a privilege with one of the things that can be a privilege. Kocourek, for example, supposes, as I have just mentioned, that a privilege is a power or a kind of power. A more traditional equation is that of *privilege* and *right*. Thus, Austin[12] on one occasion said that a privilege is the right conferred specifically on a single person or for a single case, though elsewhere he paraphrased this as 'an immunity from duty'. Hohfeld speaks of 'the privilege of self-defence' where what seems to be meant is 'the right of self-defence' and Kocourek, despite his own identification of privilege and power, maintained that there is a sense of 'privilege' equal to right.[13] Even in the cases, Luxmoore LJ's remark quoted above, which rightly linked the privilege to the exceptional, narrowed it to a right; though this may only have been as an illustration.[14] This assimilation of privilege and right is, no doubt, due to the

[10] (1930), 255; (1927), 24, 83, 125–8.

[11] (1927), 11, n. 5, 24, 83, 125–8. A further ambivalence is between the view that a privilege is a reciprocal of power, and therefore convertible with it, and the view that it is a kind of power. On the former view, they would be mutually implicative, on the latter view privilege would imply power, but not vice versa.

[12] (1861), 431; cp. Lecture IV.

[13] Hohfeld (1919), 33; Kocourek (1927), 8–9, notes 2 and 3 and glossary 439–41.

[14] *Le Strange* v. *Pettefar* (1939), 161 L.T.R. 300.

fact that many rights are privileges, that is, confined to a few classes of people, and many privileges take the form of rights.[15] Thus, Hohfeld accuses his fellow jurisprudents, Holland and Gray, of blurring the distinction between rights and privileges because the rights they quote, such as that which an owner has to enjoy his garden or a parent to chastise his children, are also privileges confined to the mentioned groups and not granted to all.

Even those jurisprudents who rightly distinguish between privileges and rights sometimes do so for the wrong reasons. Thus, one of Hohfeld's reasons for rightly distinguishing between a right and a privilege is that the correlative of someone's right, for example to keep another off his land, is another's duty, namely not to enter the land, whereas the correlative of someone's privilege, for example of entering the land himself, is another's 'no right', namely to keep him off. But though one can certainly and importantly distinguish between saying that someone has a right to V and saying that he has a duty not to V, the fact is that some rights in A (for example to assume or expect X, to allow or refuse Y) involve only the former in B and some (for example to enter a building, to walk in a park, to ask for a driving licence) involve also the latter in B. There is no more warrant in this distinction for saying that the former rights are really privileges than there would be for saying that because some duties (for example to repay my debts, to keep my promises) involve rights, whereas other duties (for example to punish the convicted, to insure one's car, not to commit suicide) do not, therefore only one of these kinds of duties is really a duty. The objection to equating rights which do not involve duties with privileges is that, on the one hand a privilege as such does not have a correlative 'no right', since it could be a privileged power, permission, immunity, etc., rather than a privileged right; and, on the other hand, a right has a correlative 'no right' as much as, or more than, a correlative duty.

[15] The suggestion of English (1973) 201–2 seems due to regarding rights and privileges as mutually exclusive.

Dias followed Hohfeld in placing both *privilege* and *right* in a table of co-ordinate notions.[16] He agrees also with Hohfeld in holding the distinction between the former and the latter notions to be, first, that a right, but not a privilege, implies a correlative duty and, secondly, that a privilege is the same as a liberty. His own contribution consists in an interpretation of various post-Hohfeld cases which I shall suggest below in fact contain neither the idea of privilege nor the idea of liberty.

The thesis that a privilege differs from a right in that the latter, but not the former, implies a duty must be rejected in the light of our earlier lengthy argument that a right does not necessarily imply a duty.

The identification of a privilege with a liberty has had some support both among jurisprudents and the law. The view was popularized by Hohfeld—followed, for example, by Dias—who held that 'the closest synonym of legal "privilege" seems to be legal "liberty" or legal "freedom" '.[17] Even Pound, who distinguishes 'liberty' and 'privilege' and sees that the latter contains the idea of 'special reasons', is inclined to group them together as 'conceptions of non-restraint' and describes privileges as 'exceptions of certain occasions and situations from the duties and liabilities ordinarily attaching to acts'.[18] Furthermore, some, but far from a majority, of the cases quoted by Hohfeld support the equation of 'privilege' and 'liberty'.[19]

The first objection to this interpretation is that not all liberties are privileges—for they may be universal—nor are all privileges liberties—for they may be powers, actions, etc. A privileged liberty is reserved for the few. The second is that it narrows the notion of *privilege* to negative privilege, that is,

---

[16] (1970), ch. 9; cf. Gray (1921), s. 25.

[17] Hohfeld (1919), 42, 47; Dias (1970), 252 ff.

[18] (1959), IV. ch. 23, s. 3.

[19] *Bourne* v. *Taylor* (1808) 10 East 189 *per* Ellenborough CJ: 'The word liberty . . . imports *ex vi termini*, that it is a *privilege* over another man's estates'. Contrast *Allen* v. *Flood* [1898] AC 1. 29 *per* Cave J.; *Matthews* v. *People* 202 Ill. 389, 401 (1903) *per* Magruder CJ: 'It is now well settled that the privilege of contracting is both a liberty, and a property right'.

the advantage which consists in being free or freed from restrictions which bind the general run of the people. Thus, Hohfeld states that 'the dominant specific connotation of the term as used in popular speech seems to be mere *negation of duty*' and also that 'a wide survey of judicial precedents' shows that 'the *dominant* technical meaning of the term is, similarly, negation of *legal duty*'.[20] The *OED* brings into its definition of 'privilege' the two kinds of form it can take. 'A privilege', it says, 'is a right, advantage or immunity granted to or enjoyed by a person, or a body or class of persons, beyond the common advantage of others; an exemption in a particular case from certain burdens or liabilities'.

(c) *Positive and negative privileges*

This twofold supposition that the dominant meaning of 'privilege' is negative both in everyday and in legal language is, as G. L. Williams has emphasized, mistaken.[21]

As regards everyday language, it may be that in fact the actual privileges that we most commonly have are negative and that the conferring of privileges most commonly consists in freeing a section of the community from the restrictions common to mankind rather than giving them additional positive advantages; but this need not be so, nor does it follow from the meaning of the word 'privilege'. What duty, for instance, am I freed from if, as the oldest man in the room, I am given the privilege of escorting my hostess into dinner or of walking in a procession behind the Archbishop of Canterbury or if, as chairman of the club, I am given a special seat in the stand, or you if, as a woman, you have the privilege of changing your mind? To have been privileged to hear Callas sing or to have had the acquaintance of Einstein is not the mere negation of a duty. Public-school boys may

[20] Cf. *Humphrey* v. *Pegues*, special exemption from burdens falling on others; *Louisville and N.R. Co.* v. *Gaines*. Fed. Rep. 3d 266, 278, *per* Baxter Assoc. J. 'Paschal says [the term privilege] is a special right belonging to an individual or class; *properly* an exemption from some duty'.

[21] (1956), 1131-2.

be a privileged class because they have better facilities and more opportunities than those in state schools, not because they have fewer duties. Nor is Hohfeld correct in supposing that 'That is your privilege' means 'You are under no duty to do otherwise'. What it means is that that—whatever it is—is something in which you are singled out from others.

Secondly, there are privileged and unprivileged exemptions. There is nothing self-contradictory in 'unprivileged absence of duty'. It is perfectly possible that everyone could be relieved of a particular duty. Everyone can be free, but not everyone can be privileged; just as everyone can be over six feet tall, but not everyone can be above average height.

A third source of this wrong emphasis on negative privilege may be the fact that if someone has something which others lack, then his possession of it may be construed as his lack of what others have. Just as a strong and handsome man lacks the weakness and plainness of others, so a privileged man is without the lack of advantages of his fellows. To be on top is to be not underneath.

Connected with this last is a further point. Some positive-looking concepts are logically negative. Perfection, fitness, and confidence, for example, indicate not so much some positive attribute, but rather the absence of defects. This is why one can be completely fit, but not completely ill; completely confident, but not completely doubtful. Illness and doubt can increase *ad infinitum*, but fitness and confidence terminate when all illness and doubt have been cured. 'Free' and 'real' are also more negative than positive. A real X is an X which is not P or Q or R, for example real diamonds are not paste, real cream is not synthetic. To be free is to be without some restriction or other, for example not to be tied up or engaged or under an obligation. This is why one can be perfectly or completely free, that is, without any restrictions.

'Liberty', therefore, is rightly defined, as we saw earlier, in terms of the absence of so and so; for example, legal liberty is the absence of any legal duty or obligation. To be at liberty to do so and so is to be under no restraint not to do it. Privilege, on the other hand, though it may in some cases consist in being free from the burdens imposed on the majority is not logically a negative term; a privilege can be a positive addition. One can be perfectly or entirely free to do so and so, but not perfectly or entirely privileged to do it. In fact, privilege is what we might call a *contrast concept*, that is a privileged X is an X which, in contrast to other Xs, has been singled out for special advantageous treatment; hence, a privileged person or class, document, communication, occasion or access, right, power, etc.

Frequently, though not necessarily, when a person is free to do so and so he is equally free not to do it. But only a mistaken assimilation of *privilege* and *liberty* would lead us to say that a company which had the privilege of granting fishing licences also had the privilege of not granting them.[22] The alleged privilege of not granting fishing licences is one which—to speak self-contradictorily—most of us have. An MP who has the privilege of presenting a petition to Parliament is free not to exercise his privilege, but he can no more properly be said also to have the privilege of not presenting a petition than all of us could be said to have this alleged privilege.

(d) Privilege in the law

As regards the actual practice of the law, Hohfeld is also mistaken in thinking that the dominant meaning of 'privilege' is negation of duty. First, as with the ordinary use, he has confused the question of the application of the term 'privilege' with its meaning. It may be that the majority of legal privileges consist in the absence of an opposite duty, as in the

---

[22] e.g. Dias (1970), 252, in his interpretation of *Mills* v. *Colchester Corporation* (1867) LR 2 CP 476; cf. *David* v. *Abdul Cader* [1963] 3 All ER 579. In fact the term 'privilege' is not used in either report. Cp. Hohfeld (1919), 47, 42-3, where he thinks that Lindley LJ's use of 'liberty' in *Quinn* v. *Leathem* [1901] AC 495, 534 is a loose way of speaking of 'privilege'; cf. his comments on Bowen LJ in *Mogul Steamship Co.* v. *McGregor* (1889) 23 QBD 59.

privilege not to testify for fear of self-incrimination or to use force in self-defence or to trespass in case of fire, etc. but this does not show that 'privilege' means absence of duty.

Secondly, it is not clear that all, or perhaps even most, legal privileges are absences of duty. What absence of duty is there when a legislature is privileged (has the privileged power) to compel the attendance of witnesses or when an MP is privileged to present a bill in Parliament or when a company has the privilege of granting licences or when someone, under the Larceny Act 1861, s. 103, was authorized to effect an arrest or in the peer's privilege of trial before the House of Lords? Parliamentary privilege in debate is more naturally interpreted as an exceptional immunity from action for defamation than as 'the absence of a duty not to utter defamatory statements'.[23]

Similarly, a large part of diplomatic privilege is an immunity from suit in virtue of which the courts of other countries have no jurisdiction to entertain an action or other proceedings against a diplomat of one country.[24] 'Diplomatic privilege', said Lord Hewart CJ, 'does not impart immunity from legal liability, but only exemption from local jurisdiction'.[25] Stone's combination of a correct insistence that 'the jurisdictional immunities of foreign sovereigns and ambassadors are essentially not freedom from duties, but freedom from the liability of having duties imposed by the judicial organs of the state' and a Hohfeldian thesis that 'a privilege is freedom from duty' would lead to a result incompatible with the ordinary legal use of 'privilege' according to which diplomatic immunities are paradigm examples of privilege.[26] What Pound calls 'conceptions of control', such as rights

[23] e.g. Dias (1970), 258; cp. Kocourek (1927), 83, on 'privileged defamation' as a privilege of declining a duty not to defame.

[24] e.g. Dicey and Morris, *Conflict of Laws*, 7th edn. ch. 7.

[25] *Dickinson* v. *Del Solar* [1930] 1 KB 376, 380; *Kavanagh* v. *Hiscock* [1974] AC 600, *per* Lord Widgery at 610 who held that s. 134 of the Industrial Relations Act 1971 did not confer a right, but a privilege which was an immunity from proceedings in certain circumstances.

[26] J. Stone (1968), 147.

and powers, can also be instances of privilege in so far as they can be limited to person or occasion, for example the right to present a bill in Parliament or the power to grant a licence.

Contrariwise, though the plea of *volenti non fit injuria* absolves a defendant from his duty, it is hardly a plea of privilege.[27]

Thirdly, what a person does may sometimes be privileged, not so much because of an absence of duty, but because he has a positive duty to do it. Thus, Lord Atkinson said in *Adam* v. *Ward* '. . . a privileged occasion is, in reference to qualified privilege, an occasion where the person who makes a communication has an interest or duty, legal, social or moral, to make it to the person to whom it is made . . .'[28] And Lord Kilbrandon in *Lynch* v. *D.P.P.* referred to the possible duty of judges to see to it that the common law changes with the requirements of society as also a privilege.[29]

Fourthly, there are many absences, exemptions, and immunities which, because they are universal to persons and circumstances, cannot be called 'privileged'. 'Fair comment' is quite a different kind of defence from 'privilege' to an action for defamation. The relation of *privilege* to *exemption* is nicely summarized by Peckham J. in *Phoenix Insurance Company* v. *Tennesee*: 'Exemption from taxation is more accurately described as an 'immunity' than as a privilege, although it is not to be denied that the latter word may sometimes and under some circumstances include such exemption'.[30]

Fifthly, Hohfeld seems to have confused the possibly correct view that having the privilege of Ving implies not having a duty to not-V—which, of course, is equivalent to its contrapositive that having a duty to not-V implies not having a privilege of Ving—with the incorrect view that not having a duty to not-V implies having the privilege of Ving—which is equivalent to its contrapositive that not

---

[27] *Pace* Dias (1970), 258.
[28] [1917] AC 309.
[29] [1975] 1 All ER 913, 943.
[30] (1895) 161 US 174, quoted Hohfeld (1919), 61.

having the privilege of Ving implies having a duty to not-V—
which would be necessary to substantiate his thesis that
'X does not have a duty to stay off the land' are 'equivalent
words' for 'X has the privilege of entering on the land'.[31]

Sixthly, many of the cases quoted by Hohfeld are cases of
liberties, powers, immunities, etc. and not, as he avers,
privileges, because there is no necessary suggestion that they
are confined to a select few. Indeed, in order to support his
thesis, Hohfeld has to accuse the courts of indiscriminately
using 'right', even when, according to him, 'the relation is
really that of privilege'. But many of the cases cited do not
support his accusation. Sometimes, indeed, Hohfeld is only
trying to distinguish between 'having a right' and 'being
exempted from a duty'—though the cases cited do not show
that the courts have confused these—but usually he is also
arguing—which the cases do not show either—that such an
exemption from duty is a privilege.

There is, for instance, nothing in the case of *Quinn* v.
Leathem to support Hohfeld's suggestion that the rights and
liberties of a British subject mentioned there—such as to
earn one's living or to deal with others—are privileges. Even
if they were privileges enjoyed only by some people, such
as British subjects or 'a trader in a free country',[32] there is
no suggestion that they are not also rights and liberties.
Some of the cases quoted make it quite plain that the rights
claimed are universal, such as the right to pursue one's lawful
calling[33] or the right to privacy,[34] whereas a few draw attention to rights and liberties which are privileged because they
are given only to a few, such as the author's right or liberty
to print his book.[35] Nor do those cases which rightly distinguish between rights and liberties always provide a reason for

[31] e.g. (1919), 39, followed by Dias (1970), 252–3.
[32] *Hilton* v. *Eckerly* (1856) 6 E & B 47.
[33] *Allen* v. *Flood* [1898] AC 1; cf. *Attorney-General* v. *Adelaide Steamship
Co.* [1913] AC 781.
[34] *Roberson* v. *Rochester Folding Box Co.* (1902) 171 NY 538.
[35] e.g. Copyright Act, 8 Anne [1709] C. 19; *Ferris* v. *Froham* (1911) 223 US
424 *per* Hughes J. at 432.

supposing that the latter are privileges.[36] Hohfeld slides from the former distinction to the latter assimilation.

Similarly, in none of the alleged cases of privilege quoted by Dias does the word 'privilege' occur, nor do they seem to be cases of privilege.[37] Neither, indeed, are they all—though some are—cases of 'liberty'. In *Chaffers* v. *Goudsmid* it was ruled that a particular MP, namely that of a member's constituency, has no duty to present to Parliament any petition which a constituent asks him to present. He is free to refuse and the constituent has no right to compel him to present it despite the fact that a citizen has a right to petition Parliament and can do so only through a Member.[38] In *Osborne* v. *Amalgamated Society of Railway Servants* it was laid down that the 'freedom' of an MP to vote according to conscience cannot be restricted by contract.[39] One can sensibly talk of the 'freedom' or 'right' which every MP has in regard to voting in Parliament, but a privilege in regard to such a matter could only be something that was restricted to some section of MPs, for example back-benchers, or some section of issues, for example on matters of conscience. In *Chapman* v. *Honig* it was not a question of a landlord's privilege or of his freedom, but of his right to give a tenant notice to quit irrespective of his motive and of whether the landlord was in contempt of court.[40] In *Musgrove* v. *Chun Teeong Toy* it was held that an alien has a 'privilege' of entering British territory, but expressly that he has neither the 'right' nor the 'licence' to do so.[41] *Bradford Corporation* v. *Pickles* was not about the Corporation's privileges, but laid down that the Corporation's 'right' to its own water did not exclude the 'right' of a neighbour to divert water on his land before it reached the Corporation's land.[42] *Cole* v.

[36] e.g. *Allen* v. *Flood* [1898] AC 1 *per* Cave J. at 29; though contrast *Clifford* v. *O'Neill* 12 App. Div. 17; 42 NY Sup. 607 (1896) *per* Adams J. at 609 and *City of Owensboro* v. *Cumberland Telephone etc. Co.* 230 US 58 (1913) *per* Lurton J. at 64.

[37] Dias (1970), 252-7.   [38] [1894] 1 QB 186.
[39] [1910] AC 87.   [40] [1963] 2 QB 502; [1963] 2 All ER 513.
[41] [1891] AC 272.   [42] [1895] AC 587.

Police Constable 443A ruled that a non-parishioner had no right to be in a church which was a Royal Peculiar and that by his ancient privileges the Dean had the 'power', 'authority', and 'right' to exclude him.[43] Neither in *Mills* v. *Colchester Corporation*[44] nor in *David* v. *Abdul Cader*[45] is there any reference to a privilege. What was at issue was whether someone who satisfied the conditions for a licence had had any right infringed by a refusal of a licence by the person who, having the 'authority', 'power', or 'discretion' to grant a licence, had refused him one.

On the other hand, though a person, who is, by the Larceny Act 1861, section 103, 'authorised' to effect an arrest, may be given a privilege, it is a privileged right or power, not a liberty. Similarly, the remark of McKenzie King in *Re Hanna*[46] that 'It is not a "fundamental human right" of an alien to enter Canada. It is a privilege. It is a matter of domestic policy', does not show, as Dias assumes, a difference between a right and a liberty (i.e. Hohfeld's 'privilege'), but between a right, which everyone would have in virtue of being a human being, and a limited permission given for special reasons.

In order to support the Hohfeldian analysis of privilege, Dias has to allege that the reasoning in many cases is at fault.[47] But, as I have already argued, neither the cases quoted concerning the rights and duties of the policeman who fears a breach of the peace nor those of trade competition nor of disputes between employer and employee provide any good reason for supposing that the courts have confused rights with either privileges or liberties.

[43] [1937] 1 KB 316; [1936] 3 All ER 107.
[44] (1867) LR 2 CP 476.
[45] [1963] 3 All ER 579.
[46] (1957) 21 WWR (NS) 400.
[47] Dias (1970), 256, n. 3; cf. 255 on *Cole* v. *P.C. 443A*.

12

Conclusion

We have now concluded our examination of the relations of the notion of *a right* both to the circumstances in which it is used and to the various other notions with which it is commonly linked in our thinking. Among the former, we have discovered, first, who or what can intelligibly be said to have a right and to what he or it can have a right, and, secondly, what kinds of answers can properly be given to the question 'What gives so and so a right to such and such?' Among the latter, we have shown its connections and disconnections with such notions as *duty, obligation, ought, liberty, power, privilege*, and *claim*.

I have argued that the possible holders of a right are fewer in kind than is nowadays frequently argued for, but that the things to which there can be a right are greater in kind than is commonly noticed. Thus, in the full language of rights —by which I mean our ordinary use of 'a right' as signifying something which one can exercise, earn, enjoy, give, claim, demand, assert, insist on, secure, waive, or surrender and which can be compared and contrasted with a duty, privilege, liberty, power, etc.—only those who can intelligibly be said to be logically capable of having these relations to rights and to duties, obligations, powers, etc., even if circumstances render them practically incapable, can possess rights. To say that something, for example a foetus, an animal, or nature, of whom it makes no sense to say it can exercise, waive, claim, secure, or surrender, a right or have a duty, privilege, obligation, power, etc., can nevertheless have a right is to stretch the ordinary notion of a right so as to blur the distinction between 'having a right' and such notions as 'being right', 'deserving' etc., in a way akin to that in which we talk of an argument, a view or objection deserving, being entitled to, or having a right to serious consideration.

By contrast, it is a common failing of theorists to base their views on narrow conceptions of the kinds of things to which one can have a right, for example the right to act or the right to receive. It is, I have argued, often the neglect of our common use of 'a right' in connection with our states, our feelings, and our attitudes which has made theories which, for example, explain rights in terms of duties and claims sound more plausible than they really are. Such theories cannot explain someone's right to be happy, to feel annoyed or proud, or to assume so and so and to expect such and such or even, as we saw, many of our rights to act or receive. Unless some proof is provided—and I have never seen any—that these are rights in some different sense of 'right', then it is a defect of these theories to overlook these examples.

Furthermore, though there are important differences between a legal and a moral right or between an institutional and a logical right to something, just as there are differences between a right to act and a right to receive, such differences, I have argued, are not differences in the concept of *right* as such, which has the same logical characteristics wherever it occurs, but are due to the ways the right is qualified, just as the important differences between, for example, what is morally, legally, and logically right or between what is morally, legally, and logically obligatory are not due to differences in the notions of *right* and *obligatory*, but to differences in their qualifiers.

None of the answers commonly suggested to the question 'What gives one the right to so and so?', that is, none of the grounds suggested for any of the rights which it is maintained we either have or ought to have, shows, I have argued, any strictly logical connection between the right in question and the basis suggested for it. All that it is possible to argue is that the suggested basis gives a non-deductive, evaluative reason for possession of the right, a reason which is, of course, often supported by common sense, our shared moral values, the apparatus of the law, some institutionalized system of regulations or conventions, etc.

The notion of *a right* cannot, I have argued, be explained either as referring to or denoting any kind of entity— though statements about rights can be true or false and, because of this, be factual—or as being equivalent to or mutually implicative with any of the notions with which it commonly keeps company, such as *duty* or *obligation, ought, liberty, power, privilege*, or *claim*. Nor can it be reduced to the notions of *right* or *wrong*. This is not to say that the notion of a right cannot be explained or understood by reference to these other notions. On the contrary, this, I have argued, is the only way to understand it. But the notion of a right is, I contend, as primitive as any of these other notions and cannot, therefore, be reduced to or made equivalent to any one or any set of them. Nor can it be explained as being a complex or system of these. To interpret the non-conceptual relations between a right and a liberty, a power, a privilege, a duty, etc. as part of the notion of a right is to make the same sort of mistake as it would be to interpret the relations between right, good, ought, duty, obligation, as parts of any one of these notions.

We saw that to say that someone has a right to V is not the same as to say that it is right to V or that he would be right in Ving, much less that he ought to V or that there is some-one else of whom it could truly be said that something would be right for him or not wrong for him or his duty to do. Nevertheless, all these notions inhabit the same area, have intimate relations to each other and have various character-istics in common.

A similar element occurring in them all is that of justifica-tion. Their differences consist largely in the object and the source of such a justification. What makes it right to V or even makes someone right in Ving or makes Ving what ought to be is commonly some characteristic either of the nature of Ving or of the consequences of Ving or even of the motives with which someone Vs, by reference to which Ving or so and so's Ving could be justified. But what gives a subject a right to V depends on something connected with him and his circumstances and not with Ving and its circumstances. He may have a right either in virtue of being of a certain kind, for example a human being, of belonging to some class, such as the class of parents or pupils, or of possessing some capacity, such as being expert or trustworthy, or some incapacity, such as having such and such needs, or of having done such and such, for example having made a contract or been given a promise, having found this or been given that, having proved or failed to prove something, or having suffered so and so, for example been the victim of an attack or of another's ingratitude, silence, or omission. By virtue of these one has a legally, morally, or otherwise favoured position in regard to that to which one has a right, whether or not it itself is right or is even something one ought to do. To have the right to V is to have something more positive than simply the liberty to V or even a claim to V, but it is not something so constraining as the duty or obligation to V, so enabling as the power to V or so selective as the privilege of Ving. Liberty opens something to me, duty or obligation closes something, power makes me capable of it, whereas a right gives me a title to it.

Whoever has a right has a title, something which entitles him, which gives him a sort of ticket of justification to do or be given so and so, to be or to feel such and such. Though the possession of this does not entail the rightness or wrongness of certain behaviour, either by him or by others, nor entail certain duties or obligations on them, it provides a strong reason, moral, legal, or otherwise, for or against such behaviour, where it would be appropriate. His right gives him immunity from at least certain sorts of criticism for what he does even when his doing this in other circumstances or somebody else's doing it in these circumstances would be open to criticism on grounds which are prima facie applicable to what he does within his rights. Moreover, his possession of a right can expose them to possible criticism for interfering or even for not helping where such interference or help is relevant. A right to V is normally linked either to some rule about Ving, for example a right to bring a guest into the club, to take a resit examination, to unemployment benefit, or to some explicitly or implicitly accepted convention, whether legal, moral, institutional, logical, etc., about Ving, for example a right to damages, to free speech, to vote, to assume so and so, or to feel proud of such and such, which the holder of a right can appeal to in order to justify his Ving. Such a rule or convention gives him a right to V by allowing his Ving a measure of exemption from criticism, objection, interference, etc. It allows him this because he or his situation falls into a certain class for which Ving is appropriate or proper or has a particular point, as when, for example, a parent, student, or driver or someone who has worked hard, has been provoked or has achieved something has a right to such and such.

The late birth of the idea of a right, which seems to have been unknown to the Greeks and possibly the Romans, as contrasted with what is right, may be partly due to the delayed, but now pronounced, prominence given to the individual. This emphasis on the individual and what he is justified in having may also explain the current fashion for translating judgements about the right treatment of babies, foetuses, animals, and even inanimate nature into judgements about their rights. It is true, of course, that the language of duties, which seems to date back to classical times, also makes the individual central, but it does so more by stressing what is expected or demanded of him than what he can himself expect or demand.

Bibliography

Aiken, H. D., 'Rights, Human and Otherwise', *Monist*, 52 (1968), 502-20.

Allen, C. K., *Legal Duties* (Oxford, 1931).

Anscombe, G. E. M., 'On Brute Facts', *Analysis*, 18 (1958), 69-72.

Arnold, C., 'Analyses of Right' in *Human Rights*, ed. E. Kamenka and A. E. Tay (London, 1978).

Austin, J., *Lectures on Jurisprudence* (1861), 5th edn. R. Campbell (London, 1911).

— *The Province of Jurisprudence Determined* (1832), edn. H. L. A. Hart (London, 1954).

Auxter, T., 'The Right not to be eaten', *Inquiry*, 22 (1979), 221-30.

Baier, K., *The Moral Point of View* (Ithaca, NY, 1958).

— 'Moral Obligation', *American Phil. Quart.* 3 (1966), 210-26.

Barnhart, J. E., 'Human Rights as Absolute Claims and Reasonable Expectations', *American Phil. Quart.* 6 (1969), 335-9.

Becker, L. C., *Property Rights* (London, 1977).

Benn, S. and Peters, R. S., *Social Principles and the Democratic State* (London, 1959).

Bentham, J., *Of Laws in General*, ed. H. L. A. Hart (London, 1970); published as *The Limits of Jurisprudence Defined* by C. W. Everett (New York, 1945).

— *An Introduction to the Principles of Morals and Legislation* (1789), ed. H. L. A. Hart (London, 1971).

— *Works*, ed. J. Bowring (Edinburgh, 1843-59).

Berlin, I., *Two Concepts of Liberty* (Oxford, 1958).

Black, M., 'The Gap between "Is" and "Should" ', *Philosophical Rev.* 73 (1964), 165-81.

Bower, G. S., *Actionable Defamation* (London, 1932).

Bradley, F. H., *Ethical Studies* (1876), pagination from paper-back edition (London, 1962).

Brandt, R. B., 'Blameworthiness and Obligations' in A. I. Melden ed. *Essays in Moral Philosophy* (Seattle, Wash., 1958).

— *Ethical Theory: The Problems of Normative and Critical Ethics* (Englewood Cliffs, NJ, 1959).

Bridge, J. W., D. Lazok, D. L. Perrott, R. O. Plender edd., *Fundamental Rights* (London, 1973).

Clark, S. R. L., *The Moral Status of Animals* (Oxford, 1977).

Corbin, A. L., *Corbin on Contracts* (St. Paul, Minn., 1950-64).

178 RIGHTS

Cranston, M., *What are Human Rights?* (London, 1973).

Crocker, L., *Positive Liberty* (The Hague, 1980).

Davidson, D., 'Freedom to Act' in *Essays on Freedom of Action*, ed. T. Honderich (London, 1973).

Dias, R. W. M., *Jurisprudence* (London, 1970).

Downie, R. S., 'The right to criticize', *Philosophy*, 44 (1969), 116-26.

Duncan-Jones, A. E., 'Authority', *Proc. Arist. Soc.*, Supplement 32 (1958), 241-60.

Dworkin, R., *Taking Rights Seriously* (London, 1977).

—— 'No Right Answer' in *Law, Morality, and Society*, ed. P. M. S. Hacker and J. Raz (Oxford, 1977), 58-84.

English, P., 'Prisoners' Rights: Quis custodiet ipsos custodes?' in *Fundamental Rights*, ed. J. W. Bridge (London, 1973), 201-18.

Ewing, A. C., *The Definition of Good* (London, 1947).

Feinberg, J., 'Supererogation and Rules', *Ethics*, 71 (1960), 276-88.

—— 'Wasserstrom on Human Rights', *Journal of Philosophy*, 64 (1964), 641-5.

—— 'Duties, Rights and Claims', *American Phil. Quart.* 3 (1966), 137-44.

—— 'The Nature and Value of Rights', *Journal of Value Inquiry*, 14 (1970), 243-57.

—— 'The Rights of Animals and Unborn Generations' in *Philosophy and Environmental Crisis*, ed. W. Blackstone (Athens, Ga. 1974).

—— 'The Rights of Animals' in *Animal Rights and Human Obligations*, ed. T. Regan and P. Singer (Englewood Cliffs, NJ, 1976).

—— 'Human Duties and Animal Rights' in *On the Fifth Day*, ed. R. Knowles (Washington, DC, 1978), 45-69.

Flathman, R. E., *The Practice of Rights* (Cambridge, 1976).

Frankena, W. K., 'Natural and Inalienable Rights', *Philosophical Review*, 64 (1955), 212-32.

Freeman, A. D. M., 'The Rights of Children in the International Year of the Child', *Current Legal Problems*, 33 (1980), 1-31.

Frey, R. G., *Interests and Rights* (Oxford, 1980).

Gauthier, D. P., *Practical Reasoning* (Oxford, 1963).

Gewirth, A., *Human Rights* (Chicago, Ill., 1982).

Godlovitch, S. and R. and Harris, J. (edd.), *Animals, Men and Morals* (London, 1971).

Goldblatt, D. A., 'Do Works of Art have Rights?', *Journal of Aesthetics and Art Criticism*, 35 (1976), 69-77.

Golding, M. P., 'Towards a Theory of Human Rights', *Monist*, 52 (1968), 521-49.

Gray, J. C., *The Nature and Sources of the Law* (New York, 1921).

Grice, G. R., *The Grounds of Moral Judgement* (Cambridge, 1967).

Hägerstrom, A., *Inquiries into the Nature of Law and Morals*, trans. C. D. Broad (Stockholm, 1953).

Hare, R. M., *Frreedom and Reason* (Oxford, 1963).

— 'Abortion and the Golden Rule', *Philosophy and Public Affairs*, 4 (1975), 201-22.

Hart, H. L. A., 'The Ascription of Responsibility and Rights', *Proc. Arist. Soc.* 49 (1949), 171-94—pagination from *Logic and Language*, ed. A. Flew (New York, 1965), 151-73.

— 'Definition and Theory in Jurisprudence', *Law Quart. Rev.* 70 (1954), 37-60.

— 'Are there any Natural Rights?', *Philosophical Review*, 64 (1955), 175-91.

— 'Legal and Moral Obligation' in *Essays in Moral Philosophy*, ed. A. I. Melden (Seattle, Wash., 1958), 82-107.

— *The Concept of Law* (Oxford, 1961).

— 'Bentham', *Proc. Brit. Acad.* 48 (1962), 297-320.

—'Bentham on Legal Rights' in *Oxford Essays in Jurisprudence* II, ed. A. W. B. Simpson (Oxford, 1973), 171-201.

— *Essays on Bentham* (Oxford, 1982).

— and Honoré, A. M., *Causation in the Law* (Oxford, 1959).

Haworth, L., 'Utility and Rights', *American Phil. Quart.* Monograph 1 (1968), 64-85.

— 'Rights, Wrongs and Animals', *Ethics*, 88 (1978), 95-105.

Henle, R. J., 'A Catholic View of Human Rights' in *The Philosophy of Human Rights*, ed. A. S. Rosenbaum (Westport, Conn., 1980), 87-93.

Hill, T. E., 'Servility and Self-Respect', *Monist*, 57 (1973), 87-104.

Hohfeld, W. N., *Fundamental Legal Conceptions*, ed. W. W. Cook (New Haven, Conn., 1919).

Holland, T. E., *The Elements of Jurisprudence*, 13th edn. (Oxford, 1924).

Holmes, O. W., *The Common Law*, 1881 (London, 1911).

— 'The Path of the Law', *Harvard Law Rev.* X (1897), 457-78.

Honoré, A. M., 'Social Justice' in *Essays in Legal Philosophy*, ed. R. S. Summers (Oxford, 1968), 61-94.

Howe, M. DeW., 'Problems of Religious Liberty' in *Nomos IV*, 'Liberty', ed. C. J. Friedrich (New York, 1962), 262-73.

Hudson, S. D. and Husak, D. N., 'Legal Rights: How Useful is Hohfeldian Analysis?', *Philos. Studies*, 37 (1980), 45-53.

James, P. S., *General Principles of the Law of Torts*, 3rd edn. (London, 1969).

Jenks, E., *The New Jurisprudence* (London, 1933).

Jones, H. W., 'Freedom and Opportunity as Competing Social Values', in *Nomos IV*, 'Liberty', ed. C. J. Friedrich (New York, 1962), 227-42.

Kamenka, E., Introduction to *Human Rights*, ed. E. Kamenka and A. Tay (London, 1978).

Kaufman, A. S., 'A Sketch of a liberal theory of fundamental human rights', *Monist*, 52 (1968), 595-615.

Kearney, R. J., 'Meaning and Implication: Other Thoughts', *Analysis*, 33 (1972), 47-50.

Keeton, G. W., *The Elementary Principles of Jurisprudence*, 2nd edn. (London, 1949).

Kelsen, H., 'The Pure Theory of Law and Analytical Jurisprudence', *Harvard Law Rev.* 55 (1941), 44-70.

— *General Theory of Law and State* (Cambridge, Mass., 1946).

Knight, F. H., 'Some Notes on Political Freedom and on a Famous Essay' in *Nomos IV*, 'Liberty', ed. C. J. Friedrich (New York, 1962), 110-18.

Kocourek, A., *Jural Relations* (Indianapolis, Ind., 1927).

— *An Introduction to the Science of Law* (Boston, Mass., 1930).

Ladenson, R. F., 'Two Kinds of Rights', *Journal of Value Inquiry*, 13 (1979), 161-72.

Lamont, W. D., *The Principles of Moral Judgement* (Oxford, 1946).

Lasok, D., 'The Rights of the Unborn' in *Fundamental Rights*, ed. J. W. Bridge, D. Lasok, *et al.* (London, 1973), 18-30.

— 'Duties of Member States of the European Community' in *Fundamental Duties*, ed. D. Lasok, A. J. E. Jaffy, D. L. Perrott, C. Sachs (Oxford, 1980), 16-32.

Lawrence, J., *A Philosophical and Practical Treatise on Horses* (London, 1796-8).

Levine, A., 'Human Rights and Freedom' in *The Philosophy of Human Rights*, ed. A. S. Rosenbaum (Westport, Conn., 1980), 137-49.

Linzey, A., *Animal Rights* (London, 1976).

Llewellwyn, K., *Jurisprudence* (Chicago, Ill., 1962).

Louisell, D. W., 'Abortion, the Practice of Medicine and the Due Process of Law', *U.C.L.A. Law Review*, 16 (1969), 233-54.

Lowry, J. W., 'Natural Rights: Men and Animals', *South Western Journal of Philosophy*, 6 (1975), 109-22.

Lyons, D., 'Rights, Claimants and Beneficiaries', *American Phil. Quart.* 6 (1969), 173-85.

— 'The Correlativity of Rights and Duties', *Nous*, 4 (1970), 45-55.

MacCallum, G., 'Negative and Positive Freedom', *Philosophical Review*, 76 (1967), 312-34.

McCloskey, H. J., 'Rights', *Phil. Quart.* 15 (1965), 115-27.

— 'Rights—Some conceptual issues', *Austral. J. Phil.* 54 (1976), 99-115.

— 'Moral Rights and Animals', *Inquiry*, 22 (1979), 23-54.

MacCormick, D. N., 'Children's Rights: A Test Case for Theories of Right', *Archiv. für Rechts- und Sozial-Philosophie*, 62 (1976), 305-17.

— 'Rights in Legislation' in *Law, Morality, and Society*, ed. P. M. S. Hacker and J. Raz (Oxford, 1977), 189-209.

— *H. L. A. Hart* (London, 1981).

— 'Rights, Claims and Remedies', *Law and Philosophy*, I (1982), 337-58.

MacDonald, M., 'Natural Rights', *Proc. Arist. Soc.*, 47 (1947), 224-50.

McLachlan, H. V., 'Must we accept either the Conservative or the Liberal view on Abortion?', *Analysis*, 37 (1977), 197-204.

Marshall, G., 'Rights, Options, and Entitlements' in *Oxford Essays in Jurisprudence*, ed. A. W. B. Simpson (Oxford, 1973).

Mayo, B., 'Human Rights', *Proc. Arist. Soc.*, Suppl. 39 (1965), 219-36.

Melden, A. I., *Rights and Right Conduct* (Oxford, 1959).

— *Rights and Persons* (Oxford, 1977).

Miller, W. M., *Data of Jurisprudence* (London, 1903).

Milne, A. J. M., *Freedom and Rights* (London, 1968).

Moore, G. E., *Principia Ethica* (Cambridge, 1903).

Morris, C., 'Rights and Duties of Beasts and Trees', *Journal of Legal Education*, 17 (1964-5), 185-92.

Morris, H., 'Persons and Punishment', *Monist*, 52 (1968), 475-501.

Narveson, J., 'Future People and Us' in *Obligations to Future Generations*, ed. R. I. Sikora and B. Barry (Philadelphia, Pa., 1978), 38-60.

— 'Animal Rights', *Canadian Journal of Philosophy*, 7 (1977), 161-78.

Nelson, L., *A System of Ethics*, trans. N. Gutterman (New Haven, Conn., 1956).

Nicholson, E. B., *The Rights of an Animal* (London, 1879).

Nowell-Smith, P. H., *Ethics* (Harmondsworth, 1954).

Olafson, F. A., 'Rights and Duties in Education' in *Educational Judgements*, ed. J. F. Doyle (London, 1973), 173-95.

Olivecrona, K., *Law as Fact* (London, 1971).

Page, E., 'Senses of "Obliged" ', *Analysis*, 33 (1972), 42-6.

— 'On being obliged', *Mind*, 82 (1973), 283-8.

Passmore, J., *Man's Responsibility for Nature* (London, 1974).

Paton, G. W., *A Text-book of Jurisprudence*, 4th edn. Paton and D. P. Derham (Oxford, 1972).

Perry, T. D., 'A paradigm of philosophy: Hohfeld on legal rights', *American Phil. Quart.* 14 (1977), 41-50.

Perry, T. D., 'Reply in Defence of Hohfeld', *Phil. Studies*, 37 (1980), 203-9.

Phillips, C. S. M., *Jurisprudence* (1863).

Plamenatz, J. P., *Consent, Freedom and Political Obligation* (Oxford, 1938).

— 'Rights', *Proc. Arist. Soc.*, Suppl. 24 (1950), 75-82.

Pollock, F. H., *First Book of Jurisprudence*, 6th edn. (London, 1929).

— *Jurisprudence and Legal Essays*, ed. A. L. Goodhart (London, 1961).

— and Maitland, F. W., *The History of English Law*, 2nd edn. (Cambridge, 1923).

Postow, B. C., 'Rights and Obligations', *Phil. Studies*, 32 (1977), 217-32.

Pound, R., *Jurisprudence* (St. Paul, Minn., 1959).

Pritchard, H. A., *Moral Obligation* (Oxford, 1949).

Rachels, J., 'Do Animals have a Right to Liberty?', in *Animal Rights and Human Obligations* ed. T. Regan and P. Singer (Englewood Cliffs, NJ, 1976).

Radin, M., 'A Restatement of Hohfeld', *Harvard Law Rev.* 51 (1938), 1141-64.

Raphael, D. D., 'Obligations and Rights in Hobbes', *Philosophy*, 37 (1962), 345-52.

— 'Human Rights', *Proc. Arist. Soc.*, Supplement 39 (1965), 205-18.

— 'Human Rights, Old and New' in *Political Theory and the Rights of Man* (London, 1967), 54-67.

— 'The Rights of Man and the Rights of the Citizen', ibid. 101-18.

Regan, T., 'Feinberg on What Sorts of Beings can have Rights', *Southern Journal of Philosophy*, 14 (1976), 485-98.

— 'An Examination and Defence of One Argument Concerning Animal Rights', *Inquiry*, 22 (1979), 189-219.

— and Singer, P., *Animal Rights and Human Obligations* (Englewood Cliffs, NJ, 1976).

Ritchie, D. G., *Natural Rights* 1894, 3rd edn. (London, 1916).

Roshwald, M., 'The Concept of Human Rights', *Philosophy and Phenomenological Research*, 19 (1959), 354-79.

Ross, A., *On Law and Justice* (London, 1958).

Ross, W. D., *The Right and the Good* (Oxford, 1930).

— *The Foundations of Ethics* (Oxford, 1939).

Ryle, G., *The Concept of Mind* (London, 1949).

Sagoff, M., 'On Preserving the Natural Environment', *Yale Law Journal*, 84 (1974), 205-67.

Salmond, J., *Jurisprudence* (London, 1902), 7th edn. 1924, 10th edn. 1947, 11th edn. 1957.

Salt, H. S., *Animals' Rights* (London, 1892).

Searle, J. R., *Speech Acts* (Cambridge, 1969).

Sesonske, A., *Value and Obligation* (Berkeley, Calif., 1957).

Singer, P., 'All Animals are Equal' in *Animal Rights and Human Obligations*, ed. P. Singer and T. Regan (Englewood Cliffs, NJ, 1976), 148-62.

Smith, J. C., *Legal Obligation* (London, 1976).

Sprigge, T., 'Metaphysics, Physicalism and Animal Rights', *Inquiry*, 22 (1979), 101-43.

Stell, L. K., 'Duelling and the Right to Life', *Ethics*, 90 (1979), 7-26.

Stone, C. D., *Should Trees have Standing? Towards Legal Rights for Natural Objects* (Los Altos, Calif., 1974).

Stone, J., *The Province and Function of Law* (London, 1946).

— *Legal Systems and Lawyers' Reasonings* (Sidney, 1968).

Tapper, C. F. H., 'Power and Secondary Rules of Change' in *Oxford Essays in Jurisprudence*, 2nd series, ed. A. W. B. Simpson (Oxford, 1973), 242-77.

Tooley, M., 'Abortion and Infanticide', *Philosophy and Public Affairs*, 2 (1972), 37-65.

Tormey, A., 'Aesthetic Rights', *Journal of Aesthetics and Art Criticism*, 32 (1973), 163-70.

Tribe, L. H., 'Ways not to think about plastic trees', *Yale Law Journal*, 83 (1973), 1315-48.

Villey, M., *Leçons d'histoire de la philosophie du droit* (Paris, 1962).

Vinogradoff, P. G., 'The Foundations of a Theory of Rights' in *Collected Papers* II (Oxford, 1928).

Vlastos, G., 'Justice and Equality' in *Social Justice*, ed. R. Brandt (Englewood Cliffs, NJ, 1962), 31-72.

Warren, M. A., 'Do Potential people have Moral Rights?', *Canadian Journal of Phil.* VII (1977), 275-89.

Warrender, J. H., *The Political Philosophy of Hobbes* (Oxford, 1957).

Wasserstrom, R., 'Rights, Human Rights and Racial Discrimination', *Journal of Phil.* 61 (1964), 628-41.

Wellman, C., *Welfare Rights* (Totowa, NJ, 1982).

White, A. R., *Truth* (London, 1970).

— 'Meaning and Implication', *Analysis*, 32 (1971), 26-30.

— *Modal Thinking* (Oxford, 1975).

Whiteley, C. H., 'On Duties', *Proc. Arist. Soc.* 53 (1953), 95-104.

Wick, W., 'Are there really "No Duties to Oneself"?', *Ethics*, 70 (1960), 158-63.

Williams, G. L., 'The Concept of Legal Liberty', *Columbia Law Review*, 56 (1956), 1129-50.

— *Criminal Law. The General Part* (London, 1961).

Williams, P. C., 'Rights and the Alleged Right of Innocents to be killed', *Ethics*, 87 (1977), 383–94.

Winslade, W. J., 'Human Needs and Human Rights' in *Human Rights*, Amintaphil. I, ed. E. H. Pollock (Buffalo, NY, 1971), 24–37.

Wright, G. H. von, *Norm and Action* (London, 1963).

Wringe, C. A., *Children's Rights* (London, 1981).

Zink, S., *The Concepts of Ethics* (London, 1962).

Index

This does not contain names mentioned only in the footnotes or the bibliography.